This learn to write workbook belongs to:

Trace Your Lines

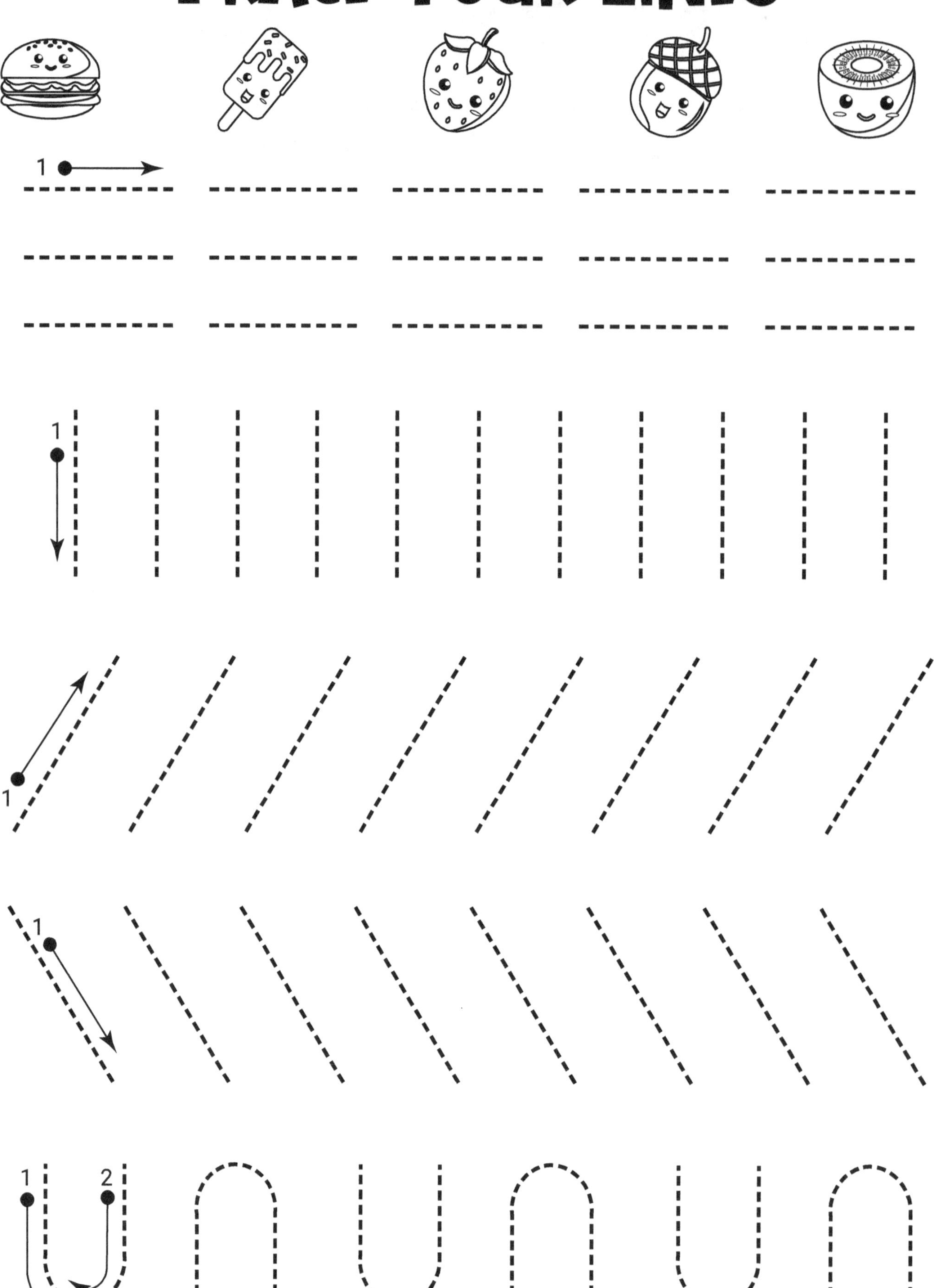

Trace Your Swiggles

AGAIN . . .

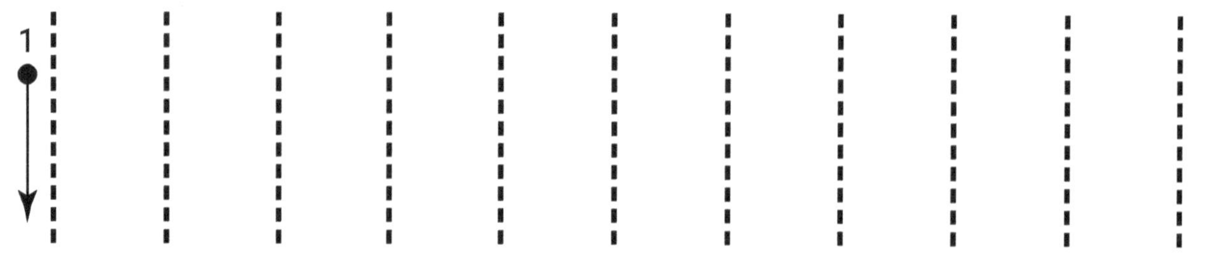

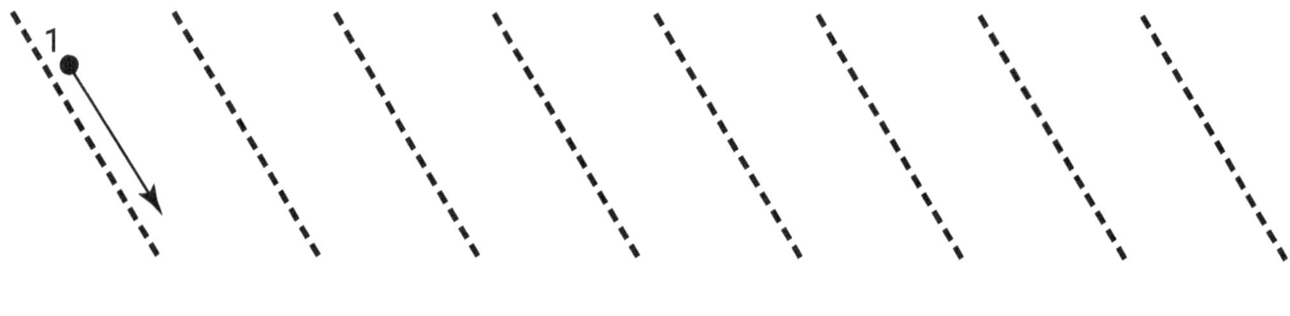

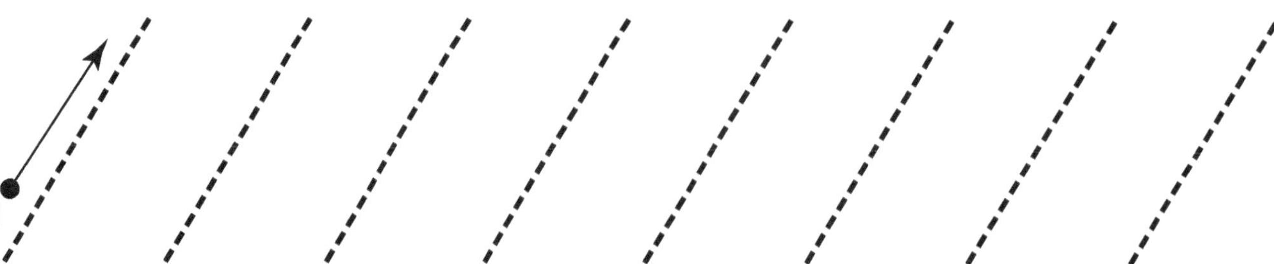

AGAIN . . .

APPLE

A

Aa

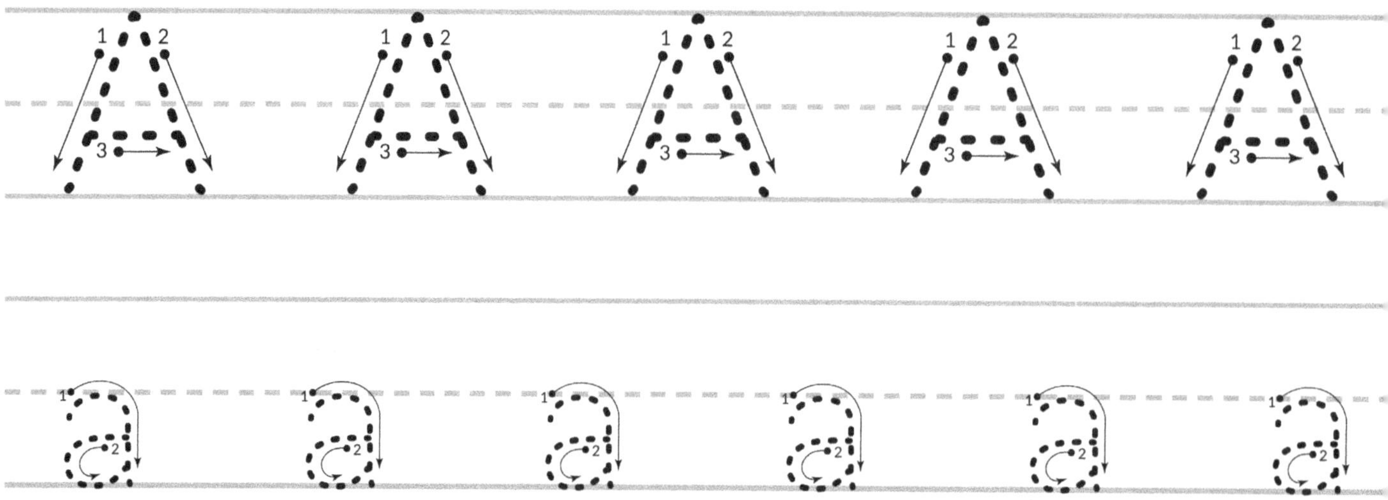

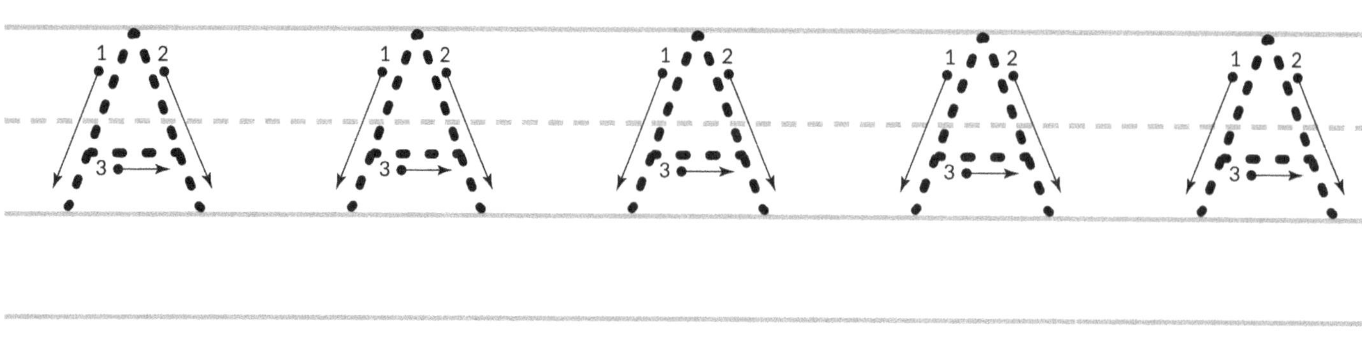

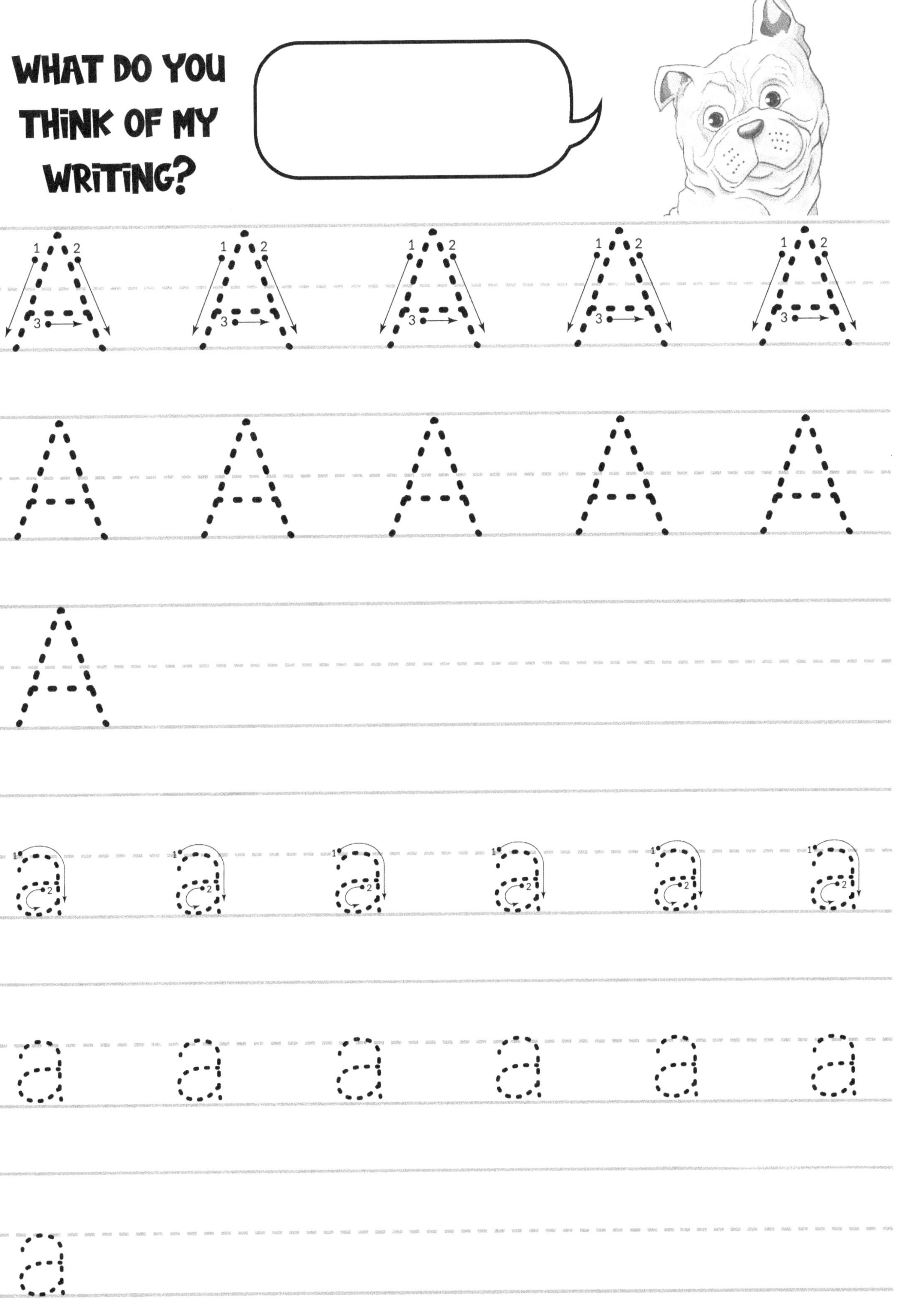

WHAT DO YOU THINK OF MY WRITING?

BANANA

Bb

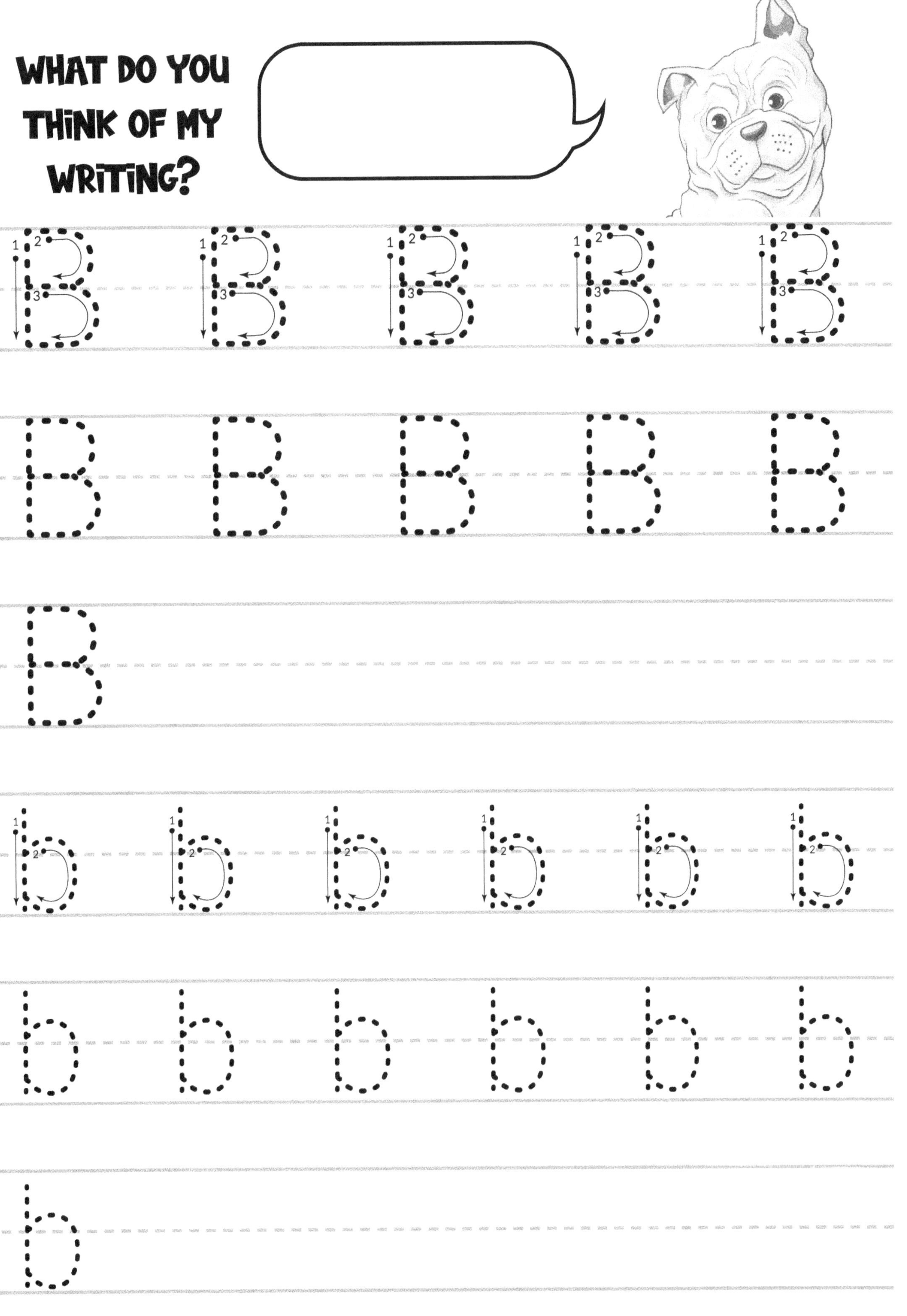

WHAT DO YOU THINK OF MY WRITING?

CAT

C

Cc

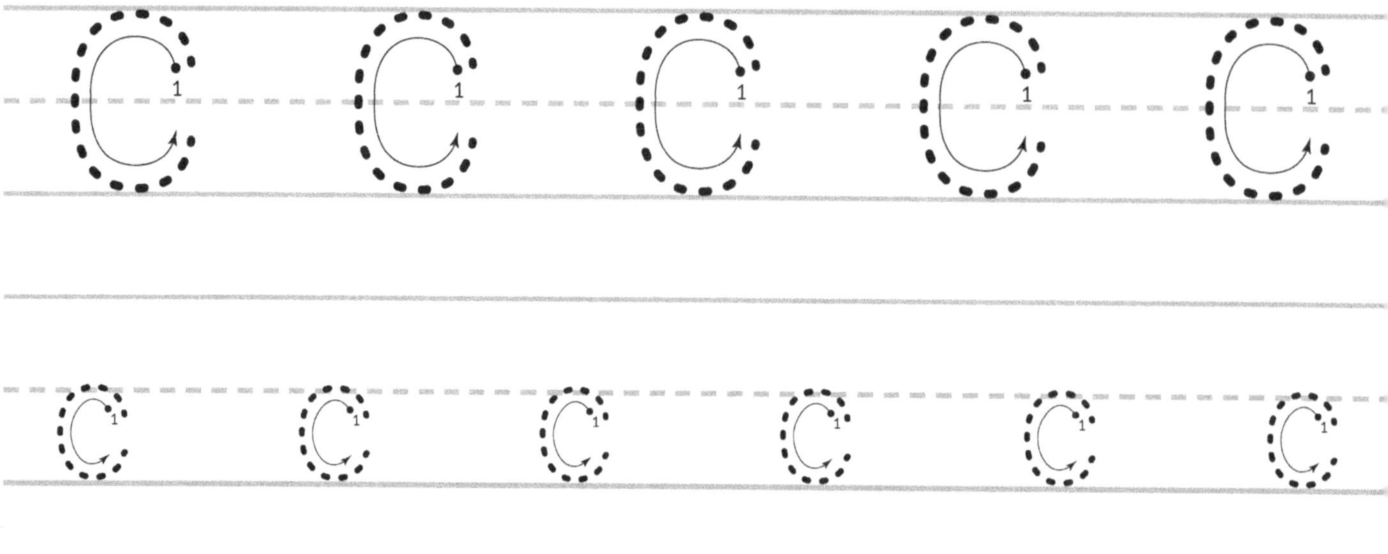

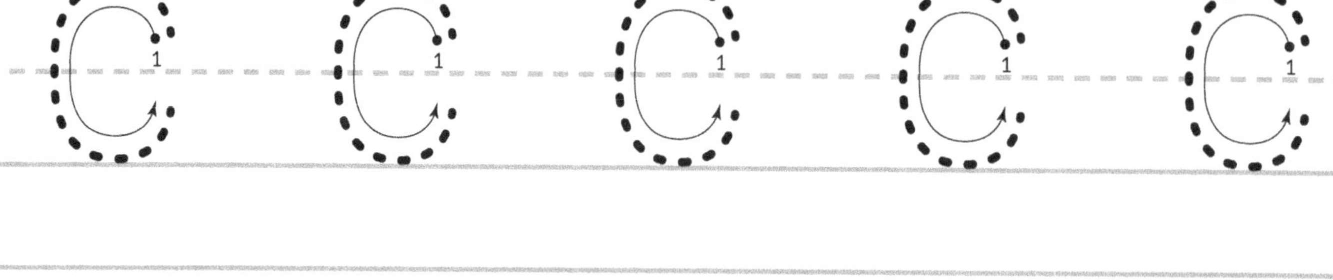

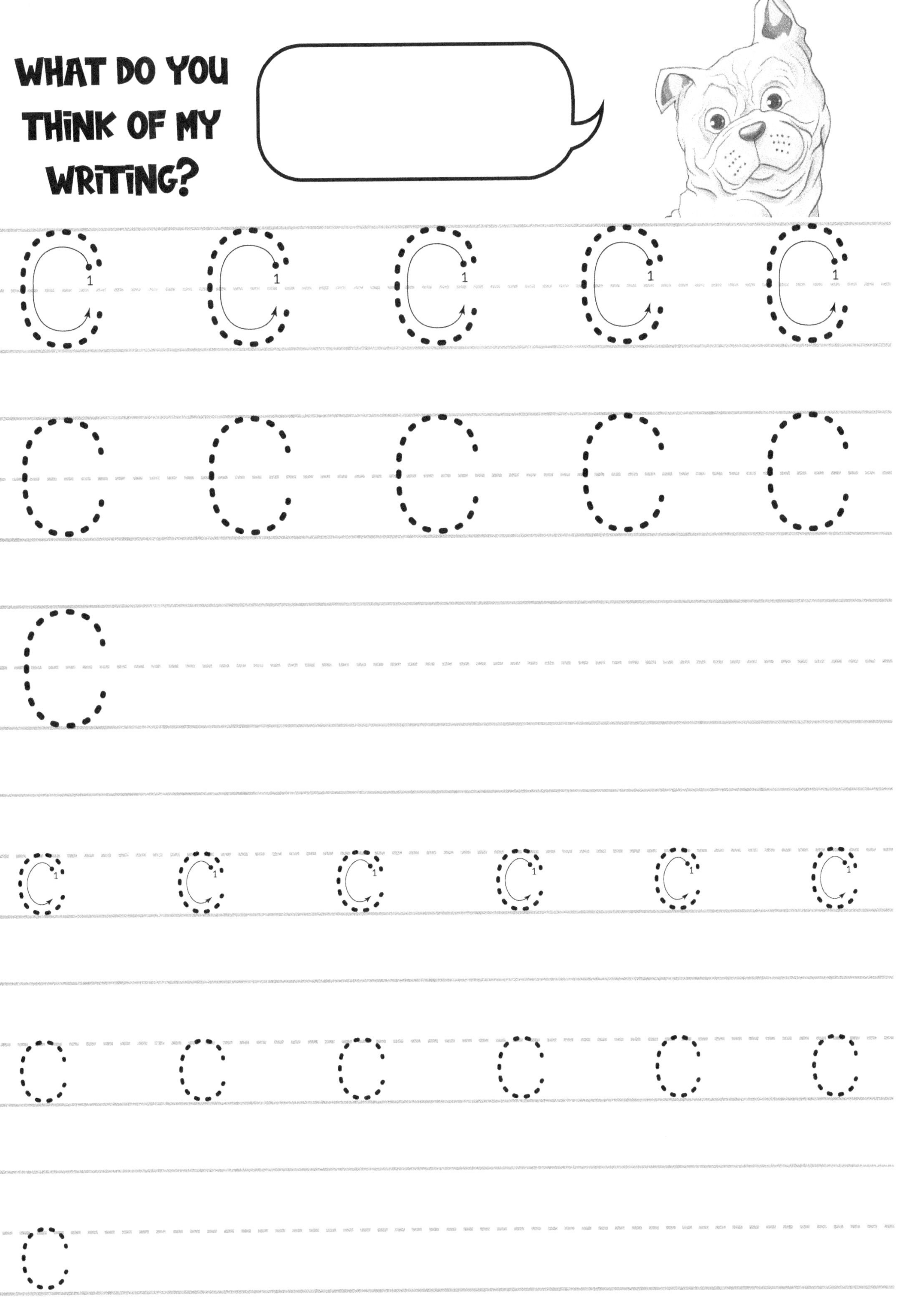

WHAT DO YOU THINK OF MY WRITING?

DOG

D

Dd

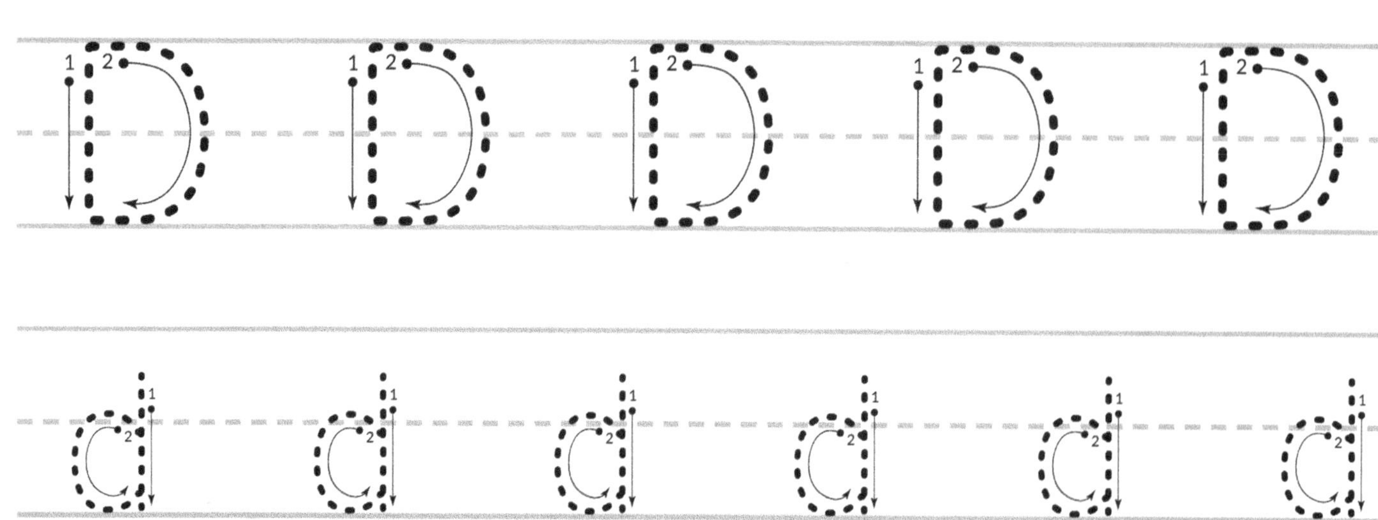

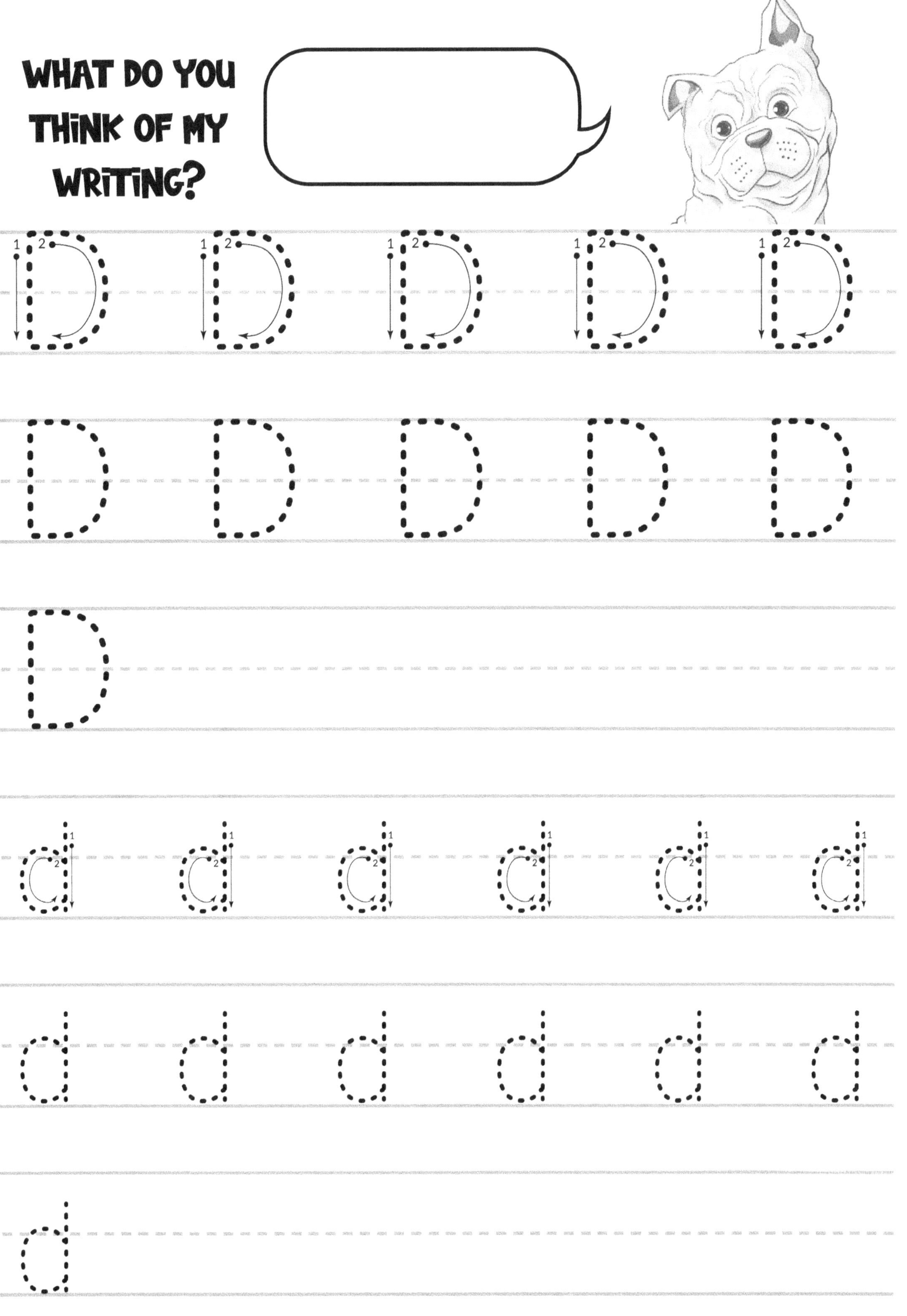
WHAT DO YOU THINK OF MY WRITING?
1 2
1 2
1 2
1 2
1 2
1
2
1
2
1
2
1
2
1
2
1
2

ELEPHANT

Ee

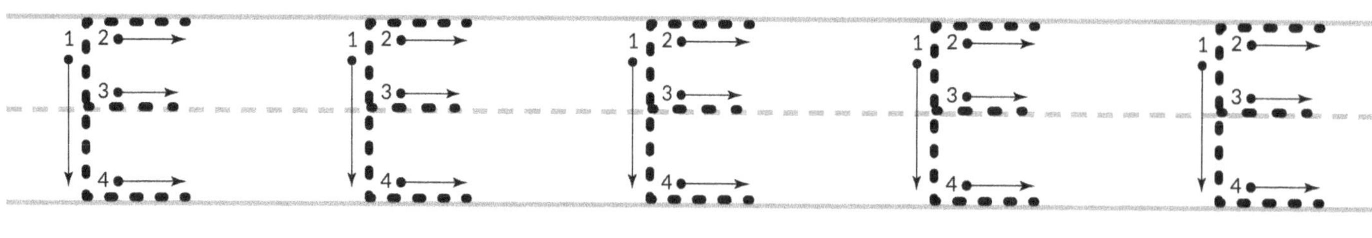

WHAT DO YOU THINK OF MY WRITING?

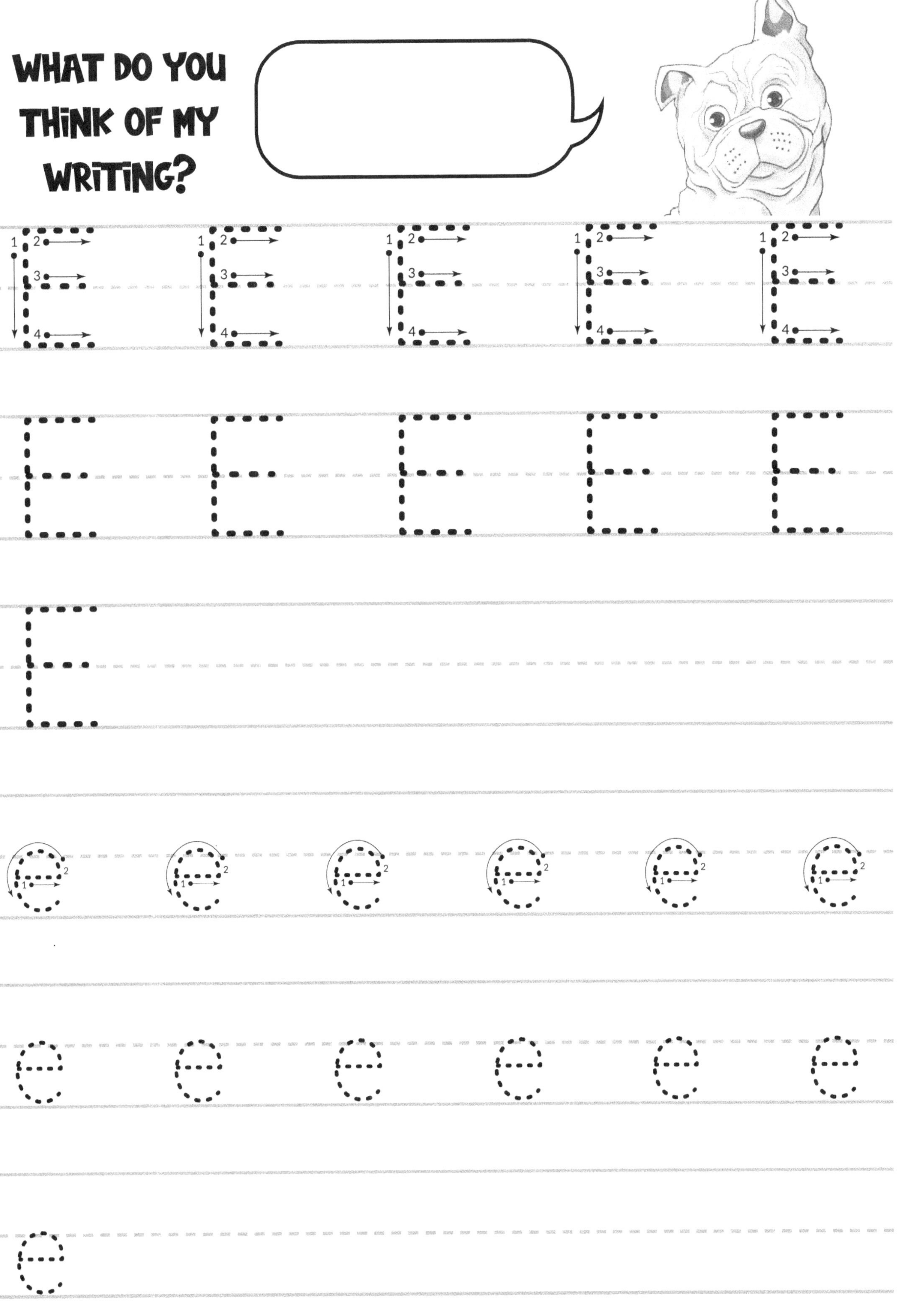

FROG

F

Ff

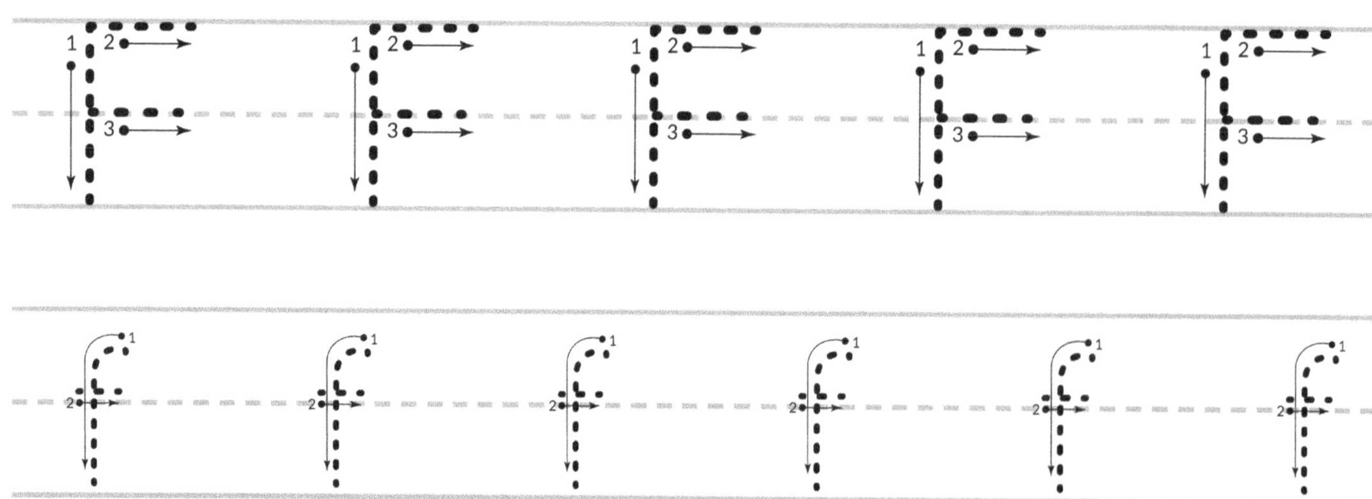

WHAT DO YOU THINK OF MY WRITING?

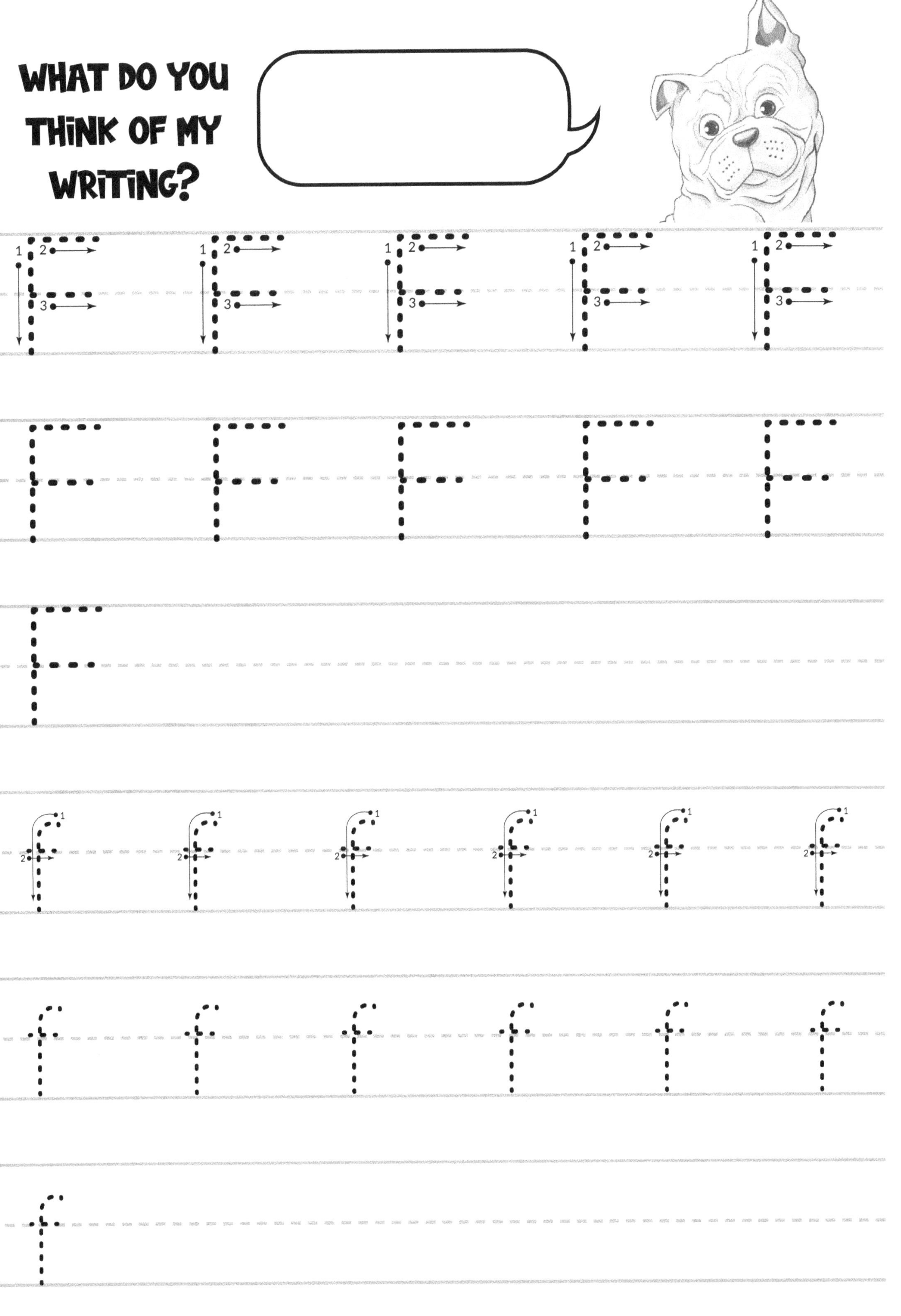

GOAT
G g

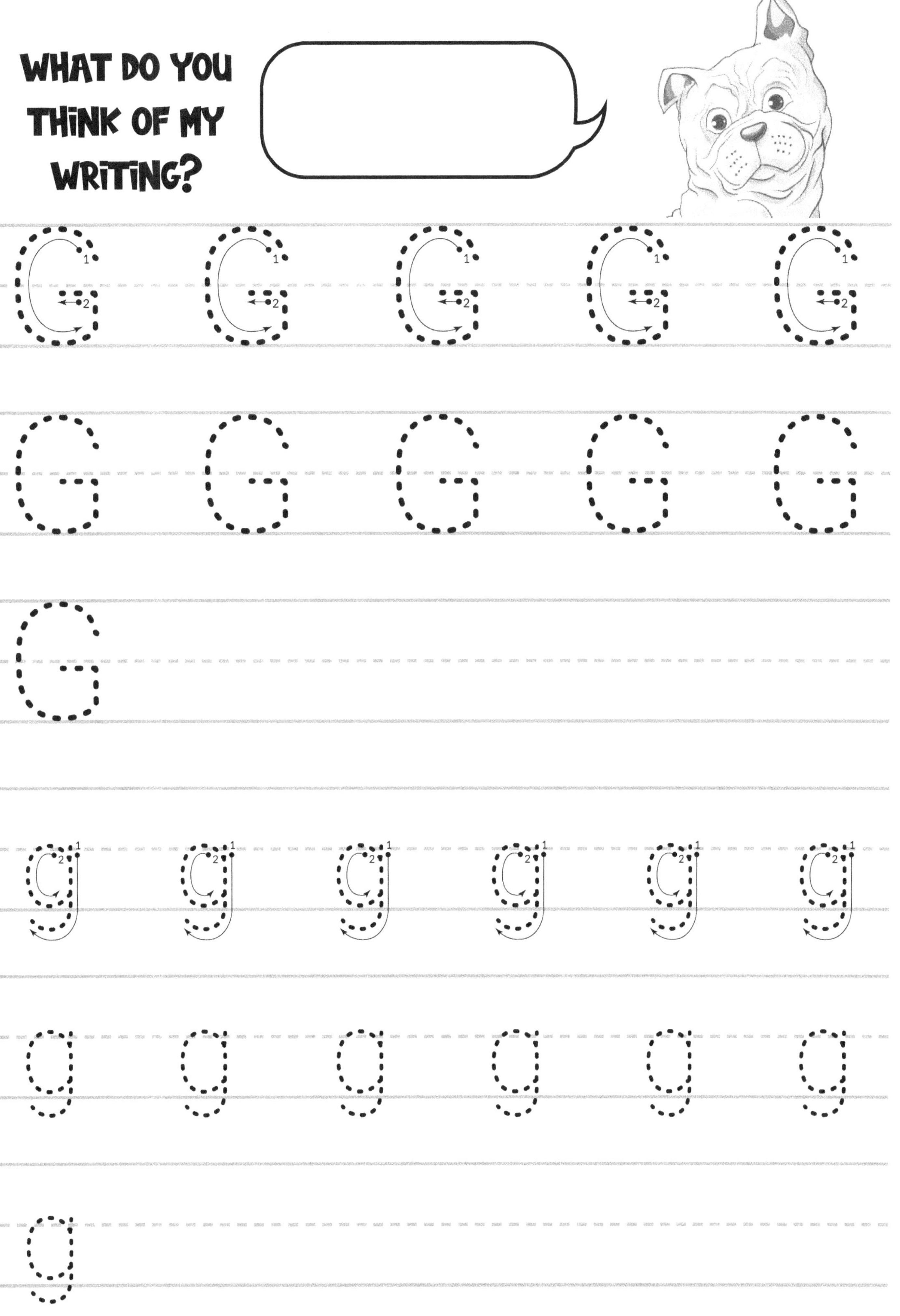

WHAT DO YOU THINK OF MY WRITING?

HAMBURGER

H

Hh

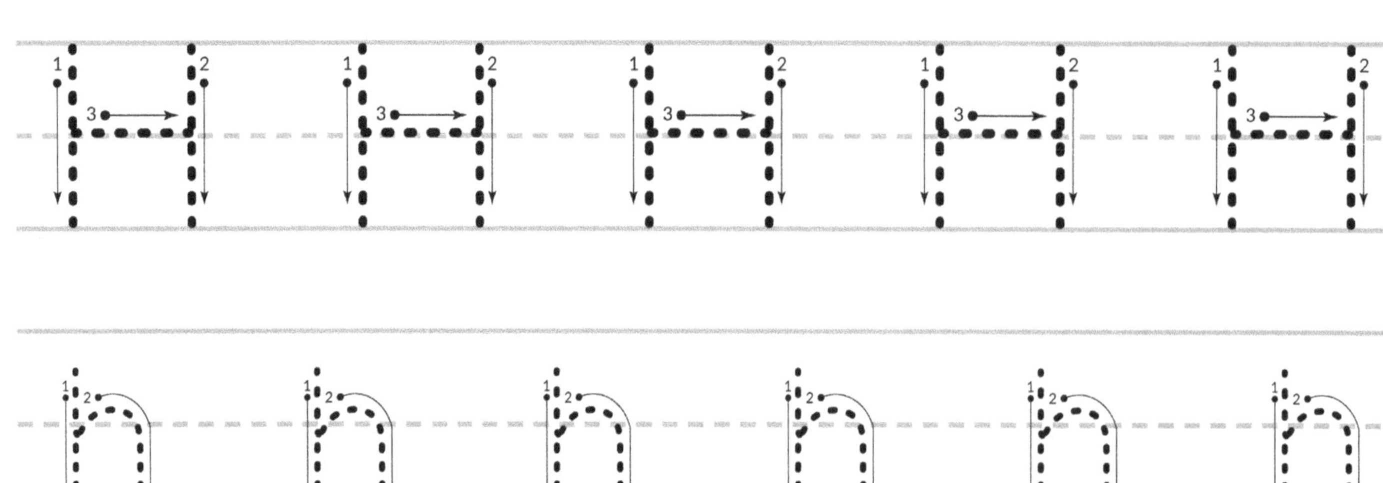

WHAT DO YOU THINK OF MY WRITING?

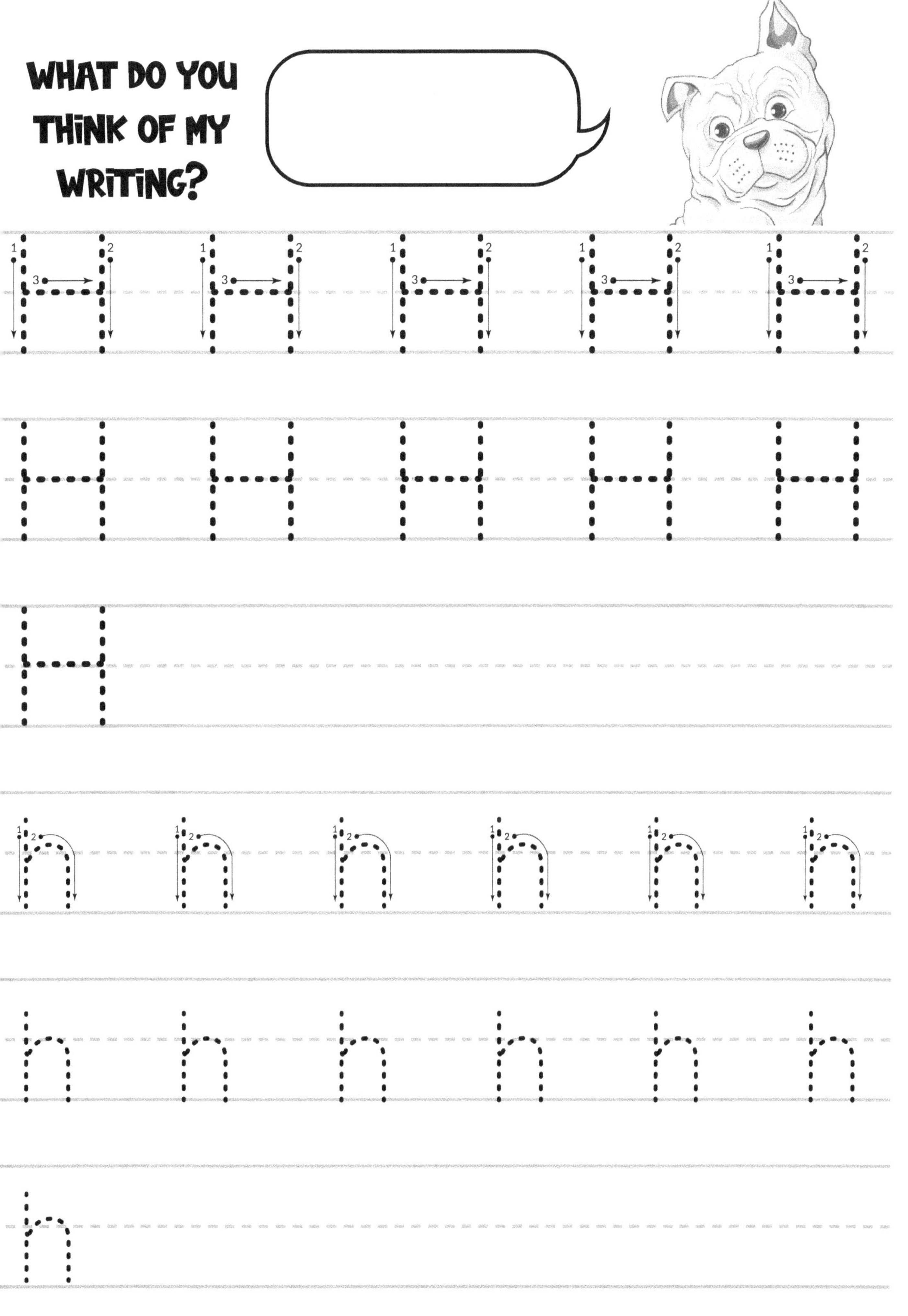

ICE CREAM

I i

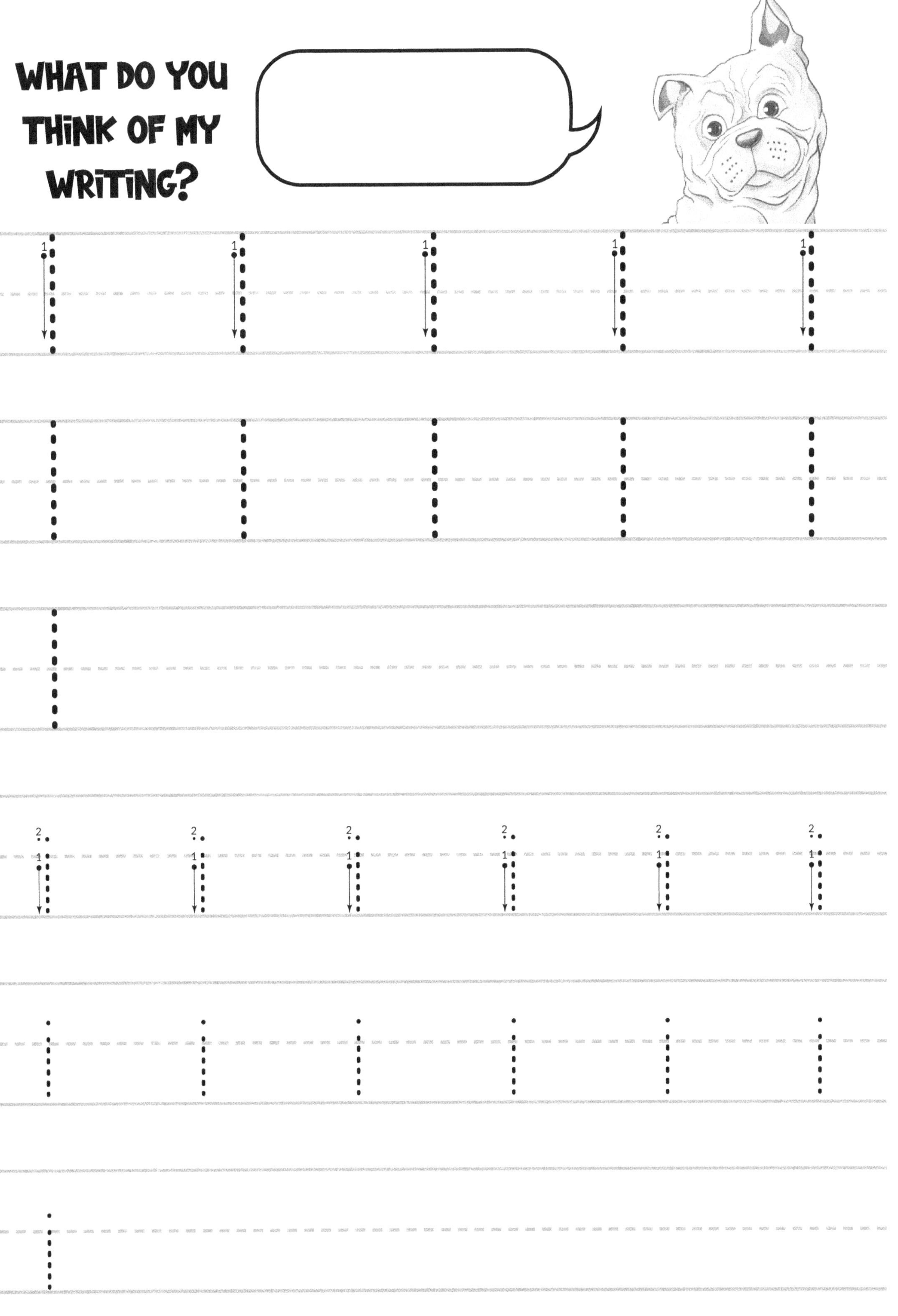
WHAT DO YOU THINK OF MY WRITING?

JELLYFISH

Jj

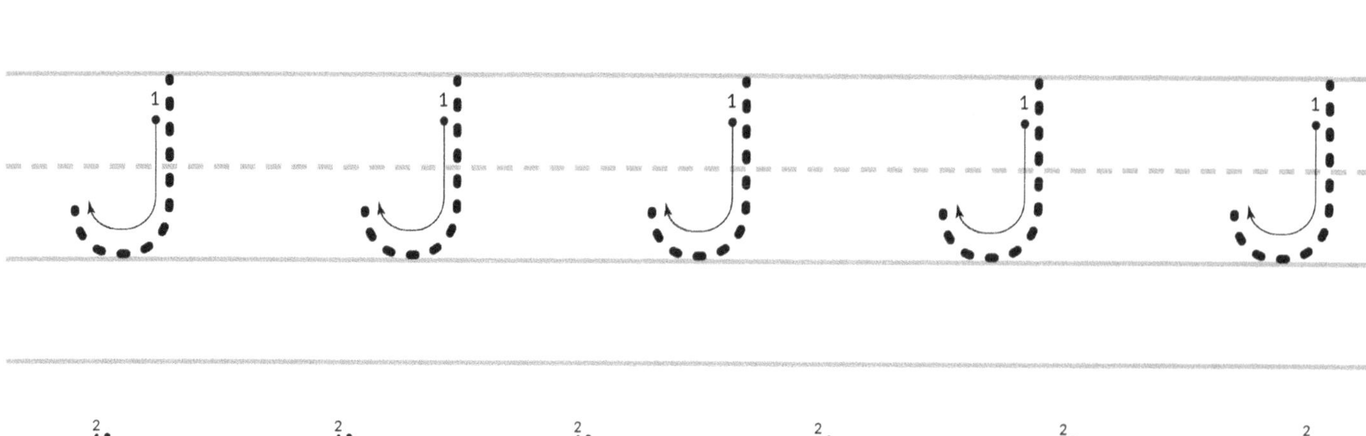

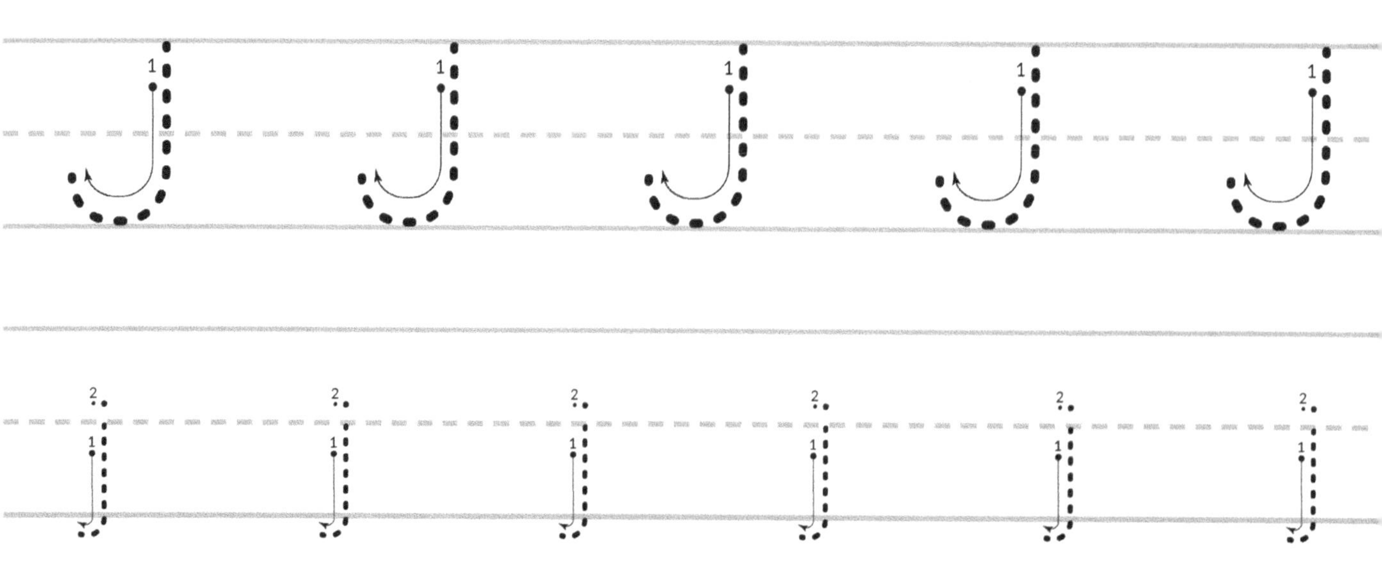

WHAT DO YOU THINK OF MY WRITING?

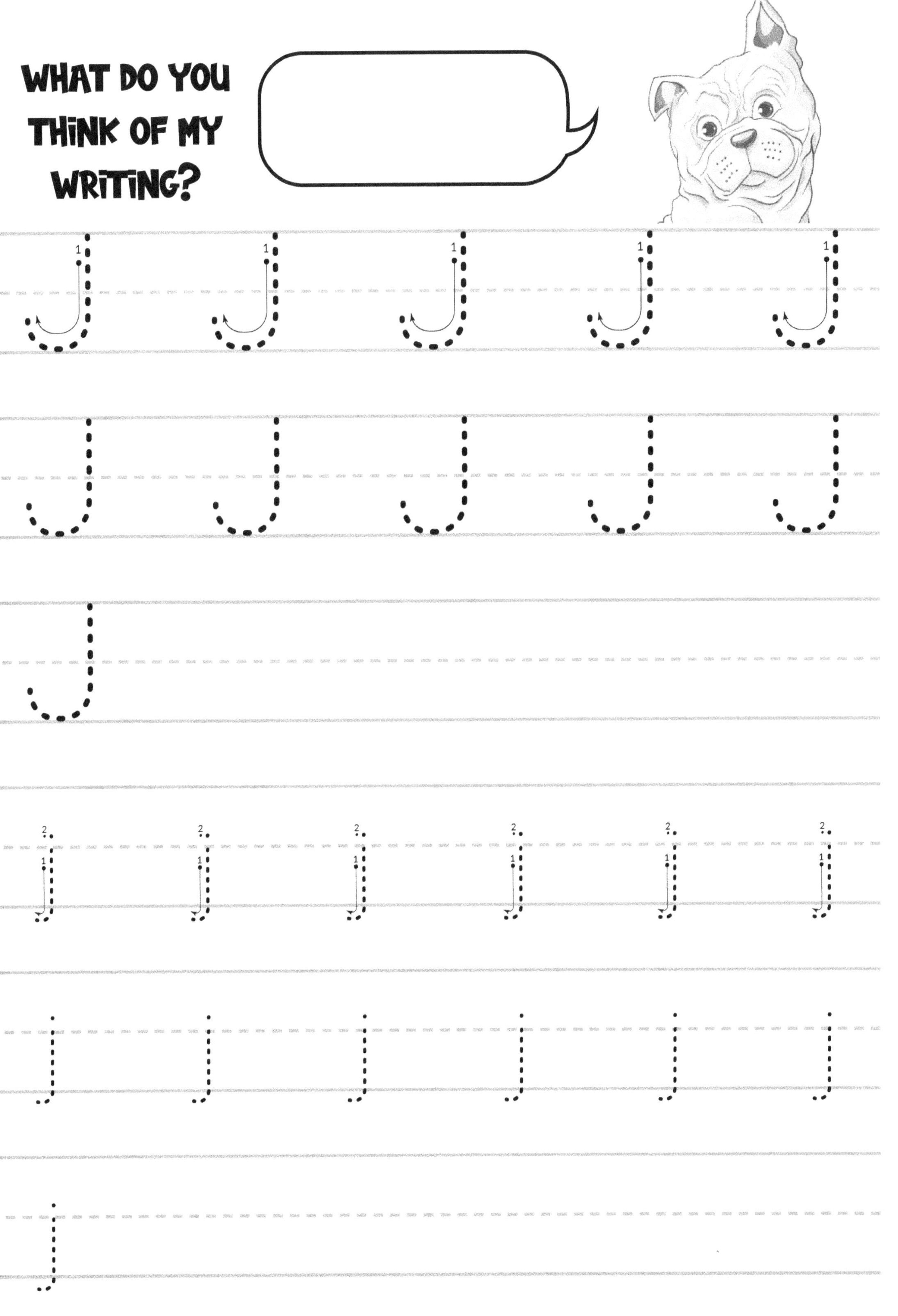

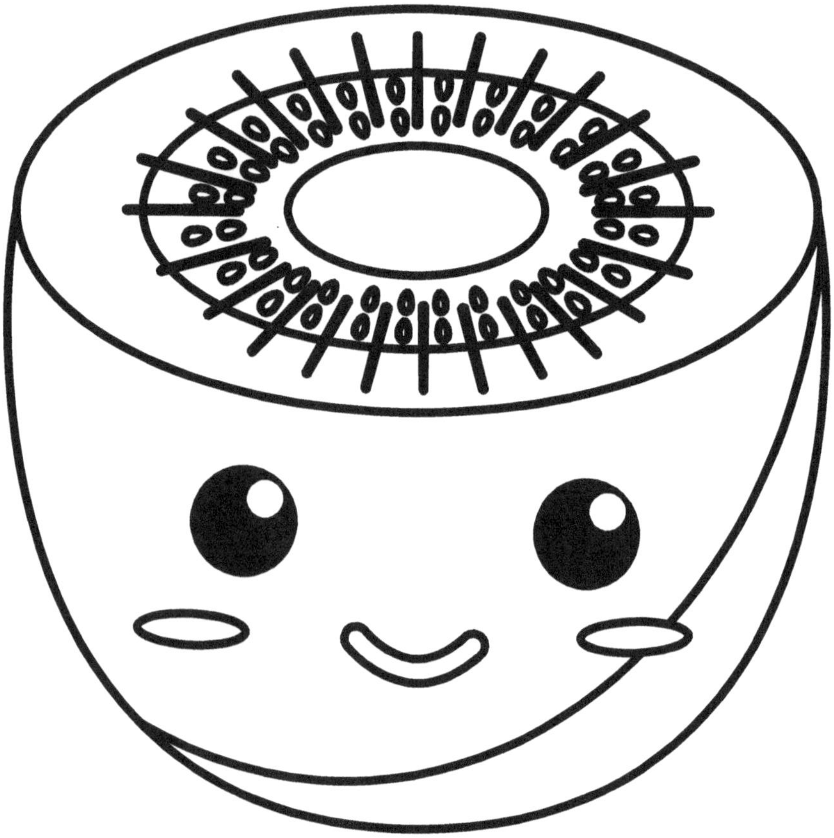

Kiwi

K

Kk

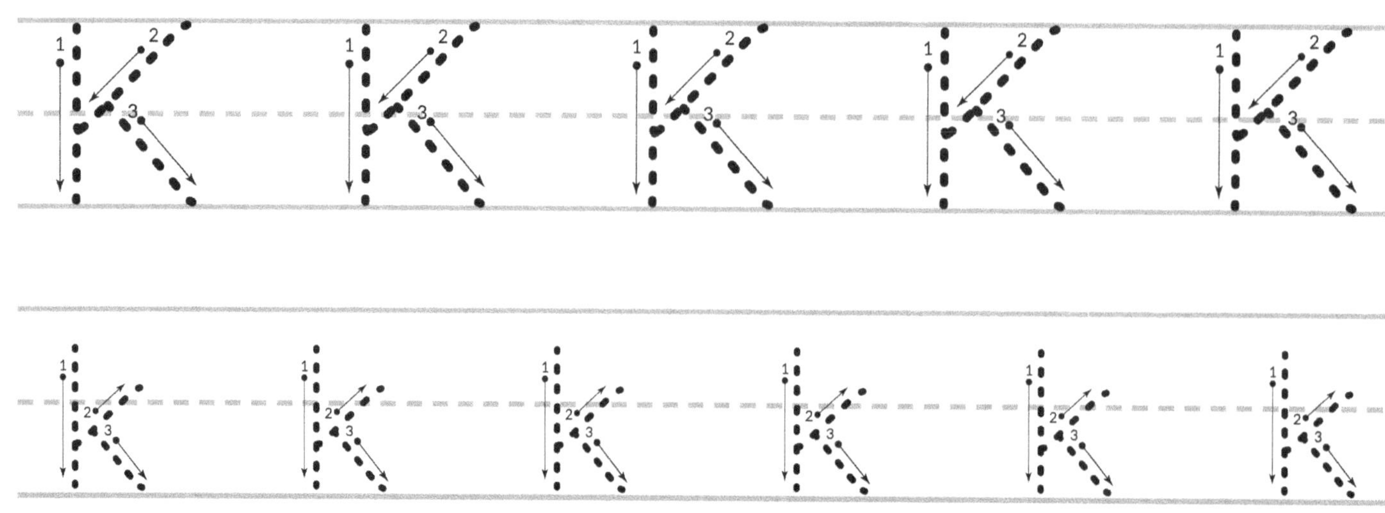

WHAT DO YOU THINK OF MY WRITING?

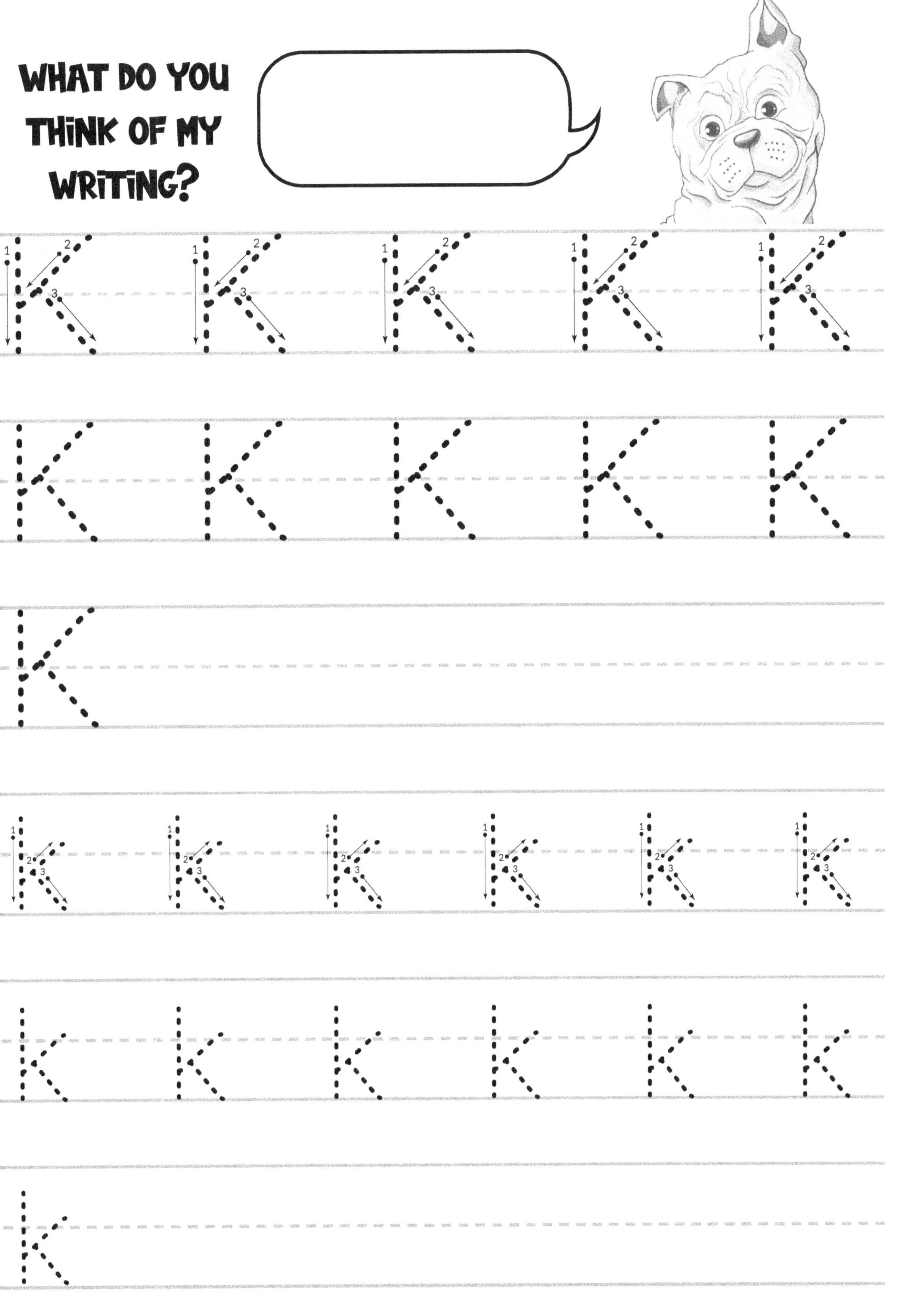

LiON
L
Ll
1
2
1
2
1
2
1
2
1
2
1
1
1
1
1
1

WHAT DO YOU THINK OF MY WRITING?

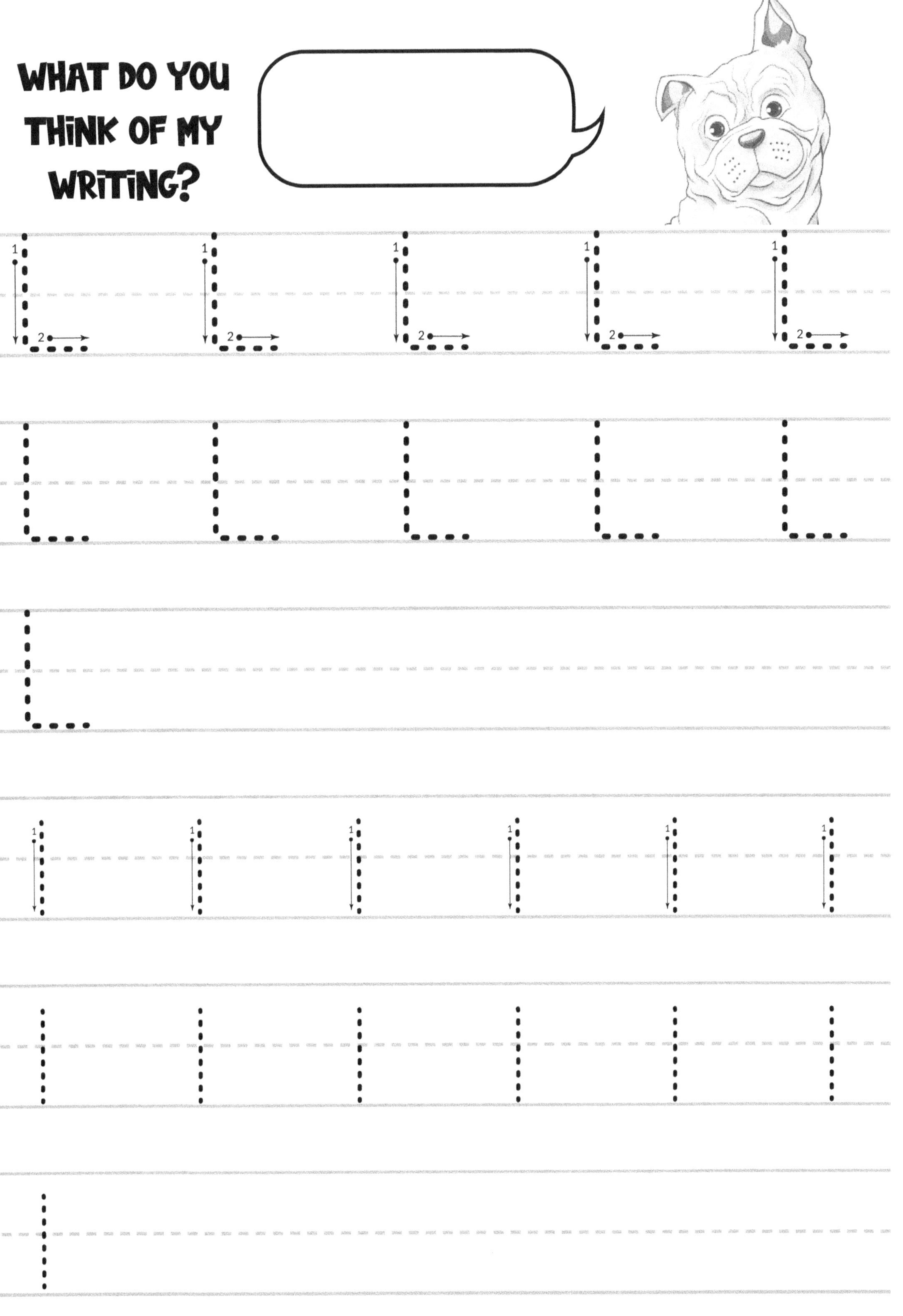

MONKEY

M

Mm

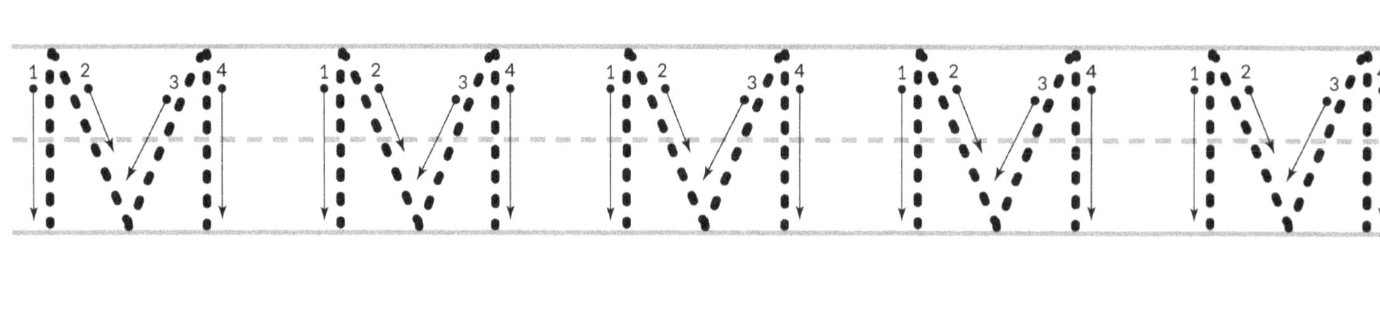

WHAT DO YOU THINK OF MY WRITING?

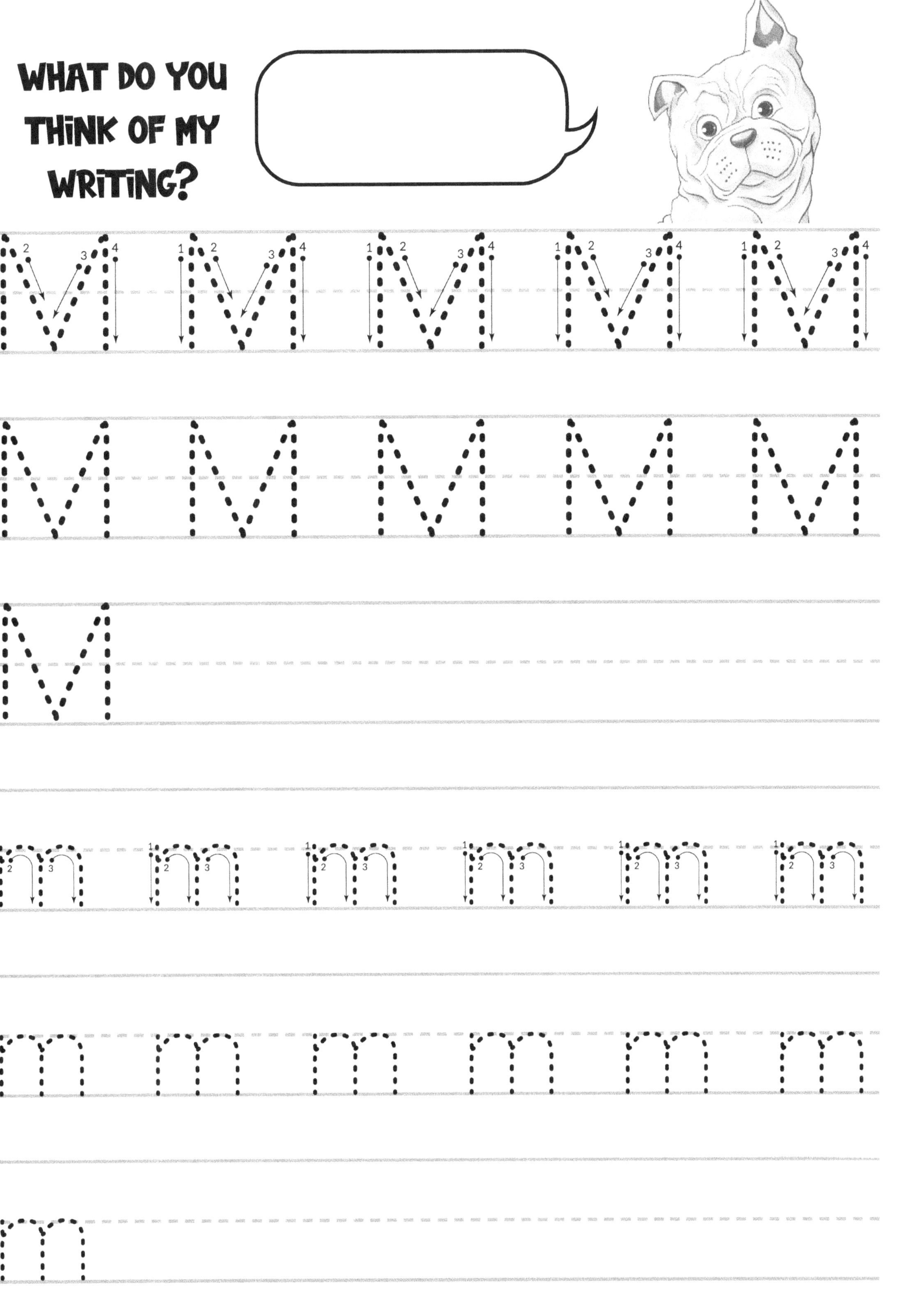

Nut

N

Nn

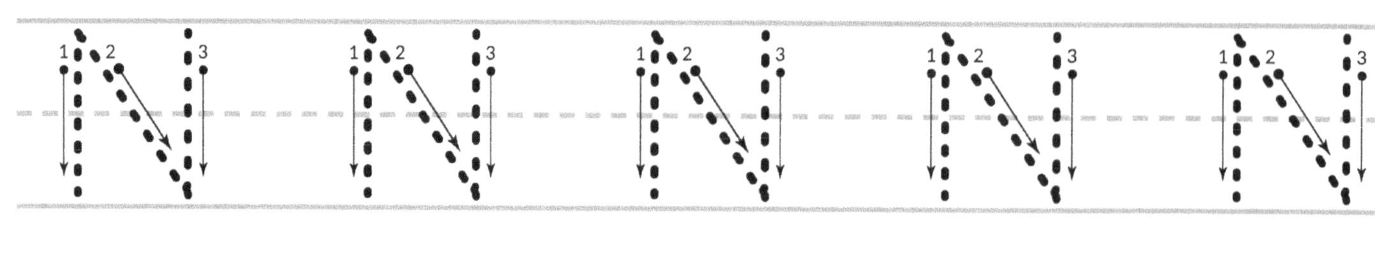

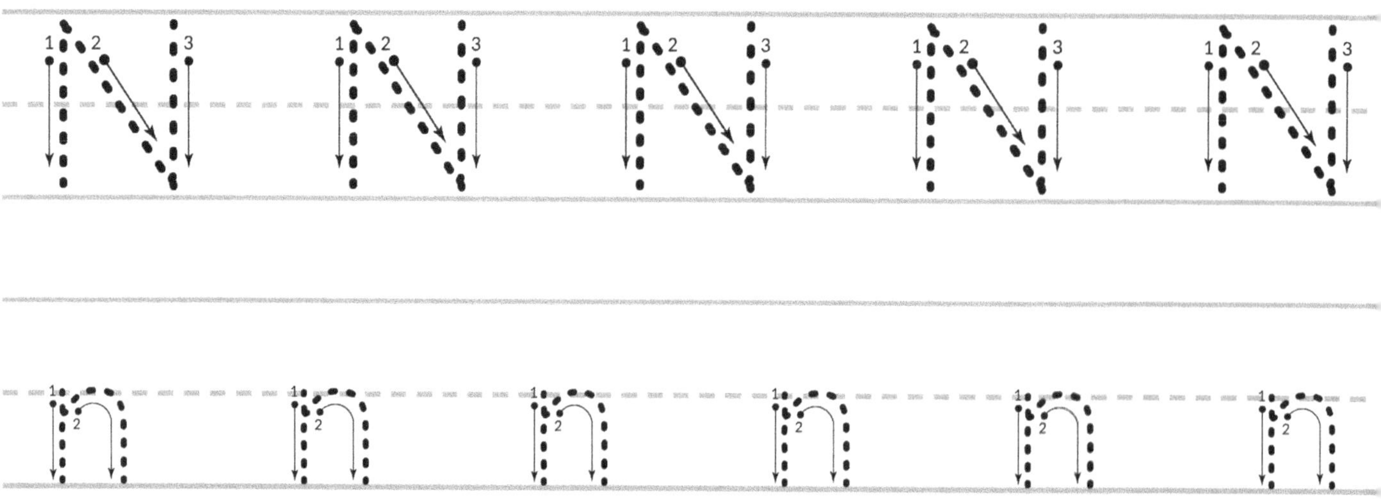

WHAT DO YOU THINK OF MY WRITING?

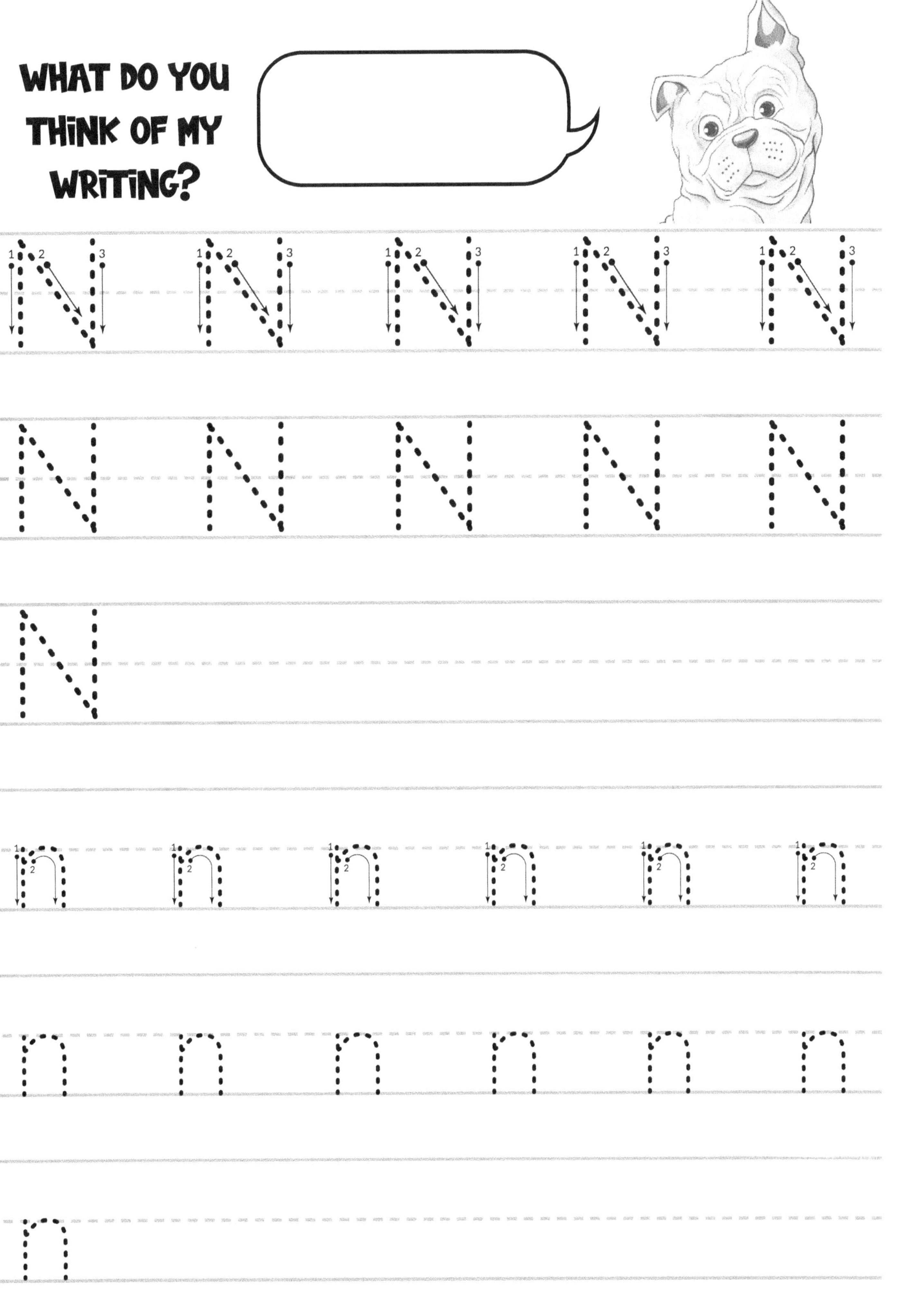

ORANGE
Oo

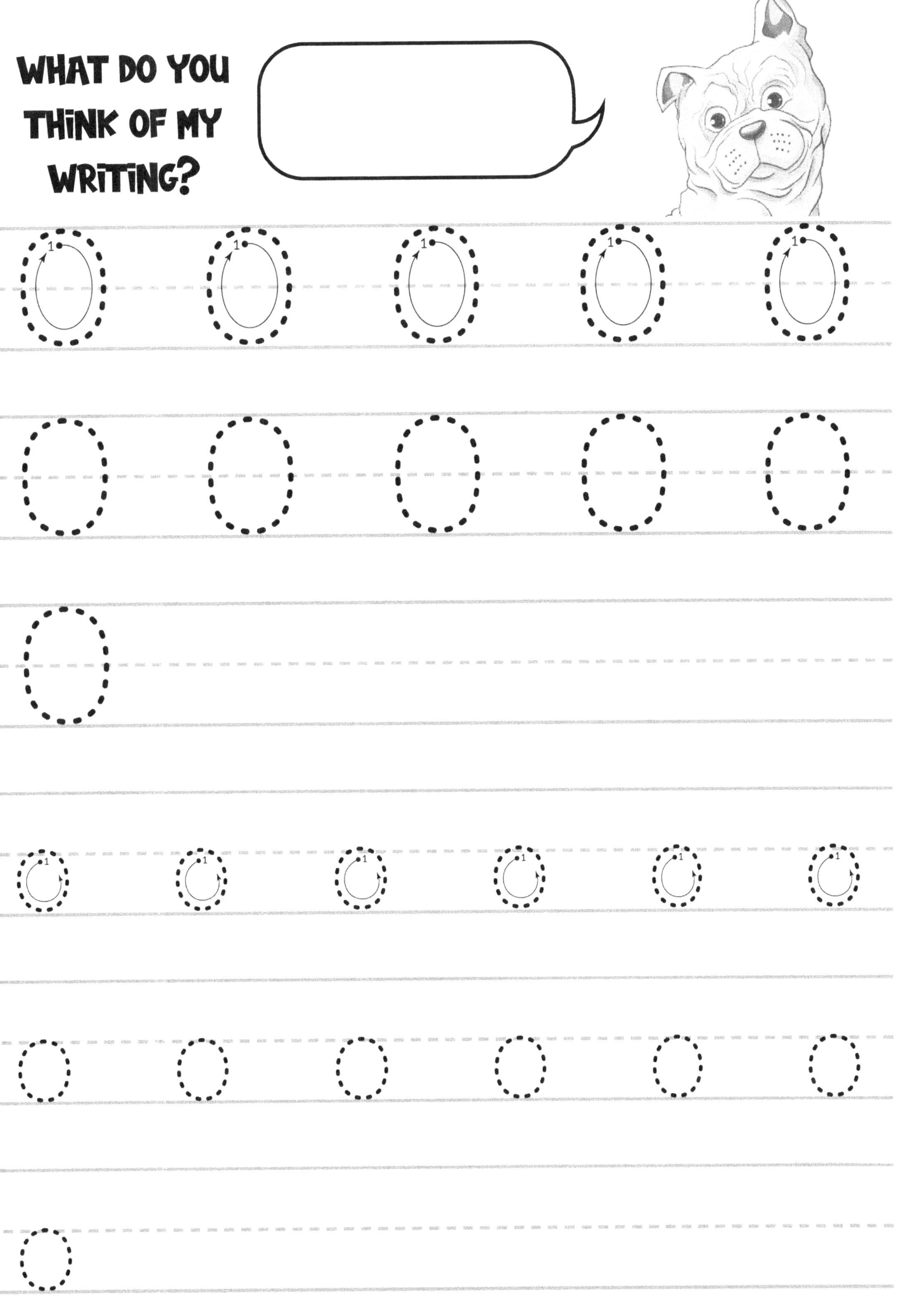

WHAT DO YOU THINK OF MY WRITING?

PANDA

P

Pp

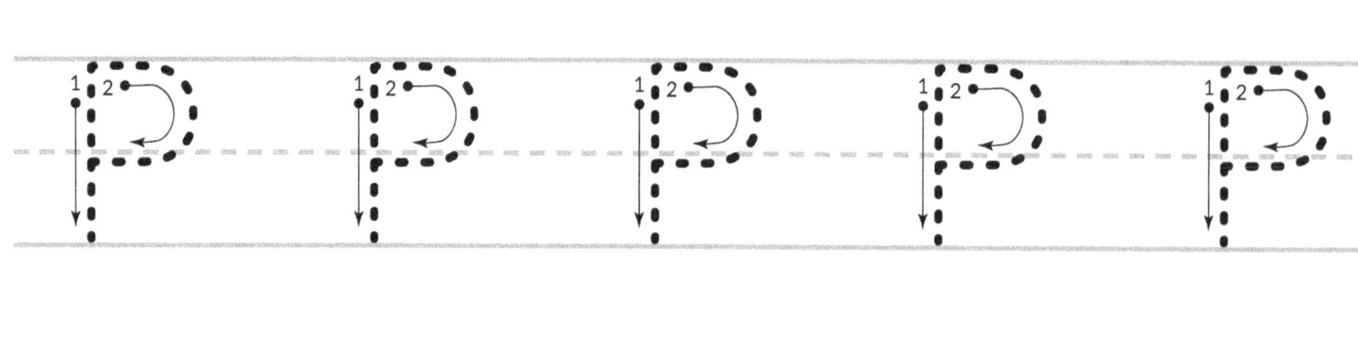

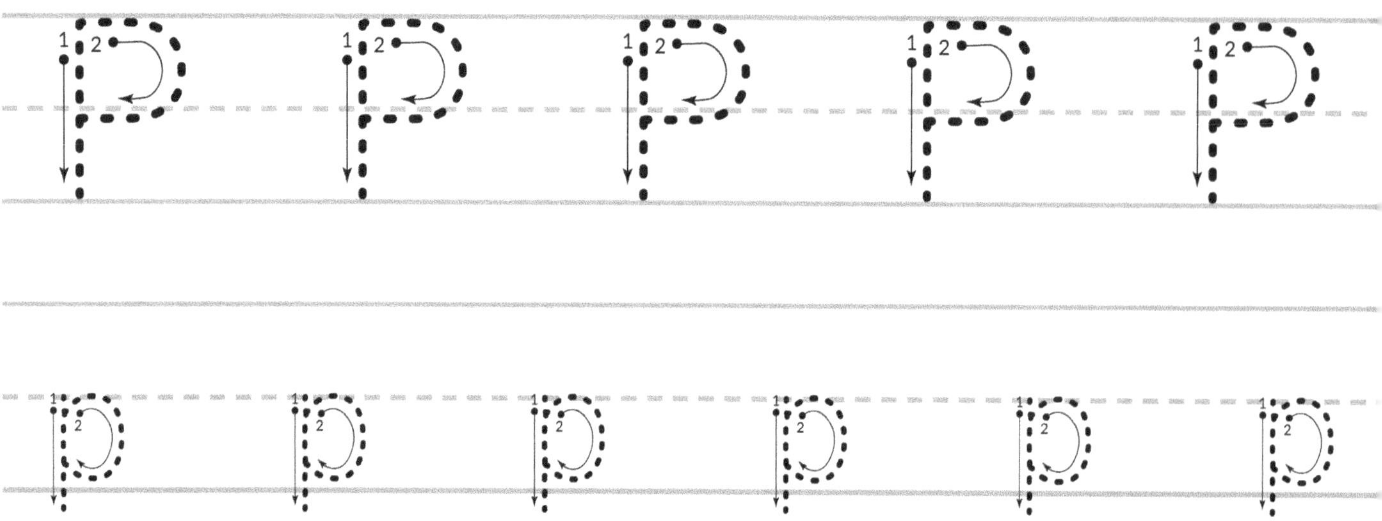

WHAT DO YOU THINK OF MY WRITING?

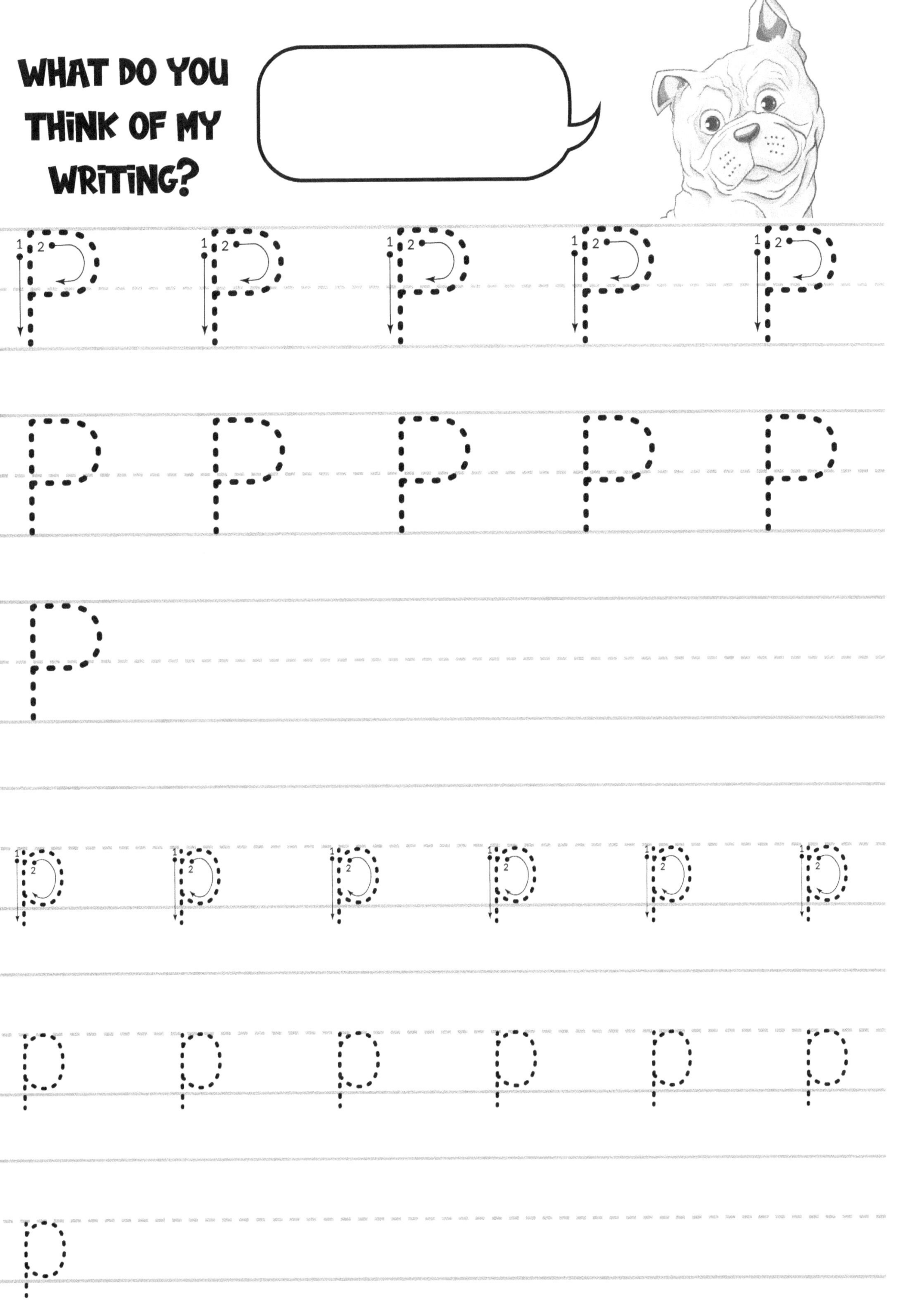

QUEEN
Q
Qq

WHAT DO YOU THINK OF MY WRITING?

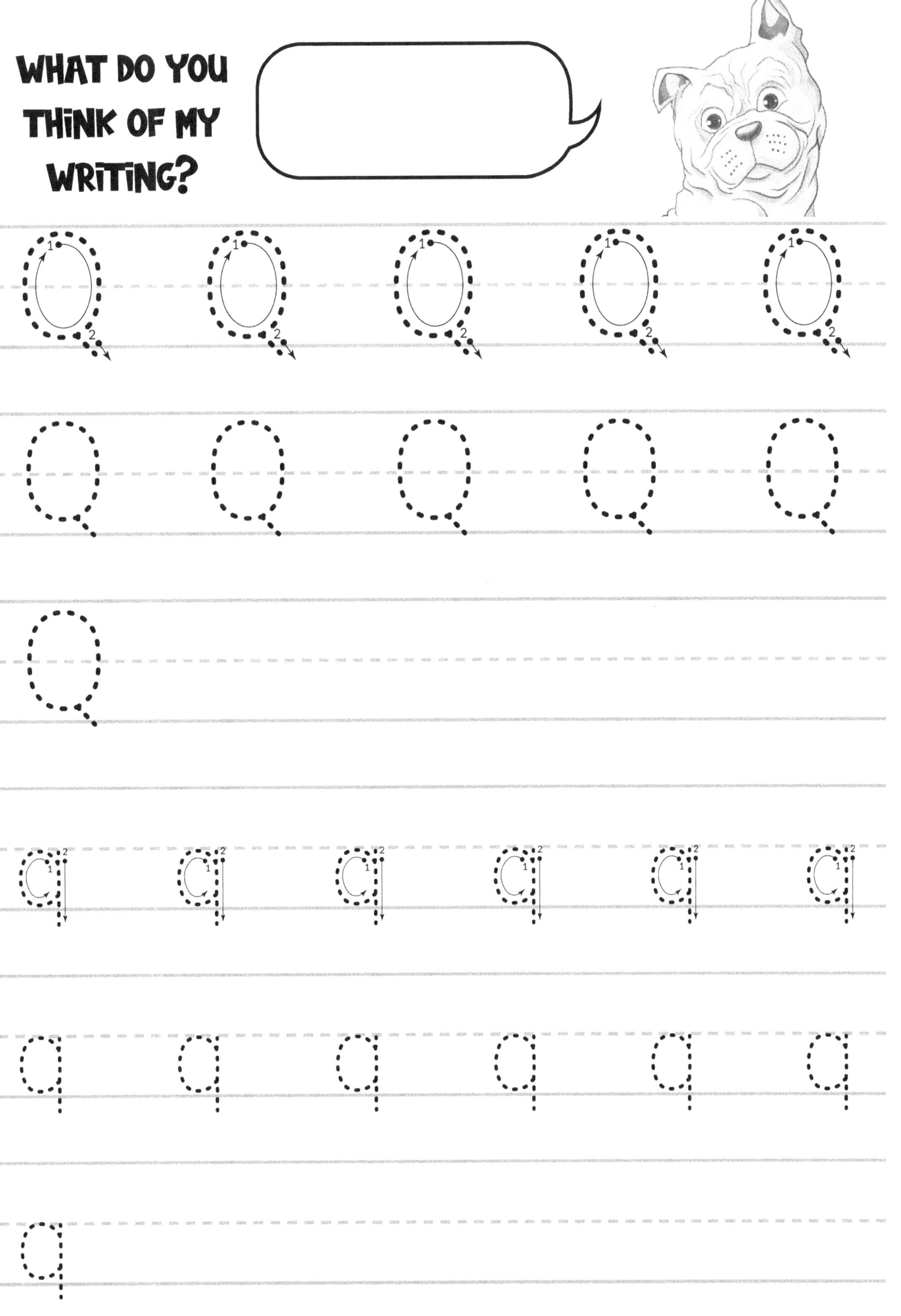

RABBIT

R

Rr

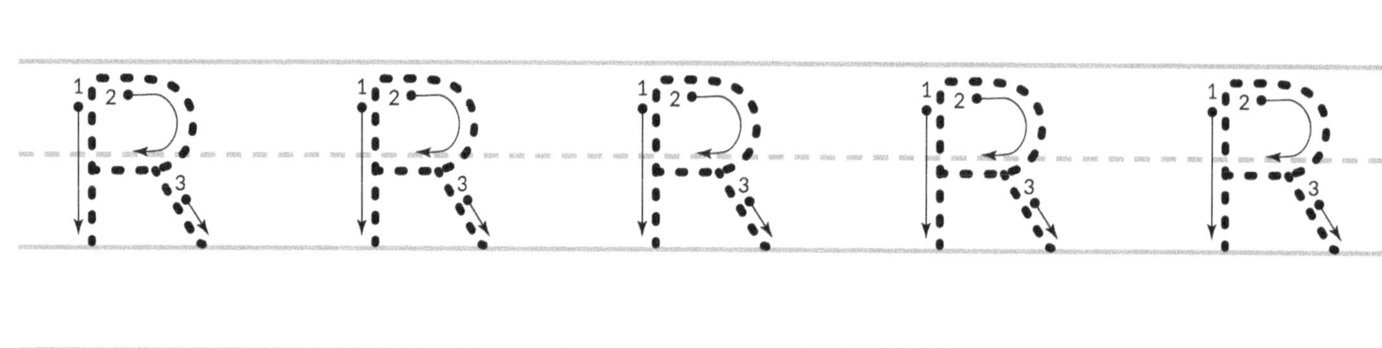

WHAT DO YOU THINK OF MY WRITING?

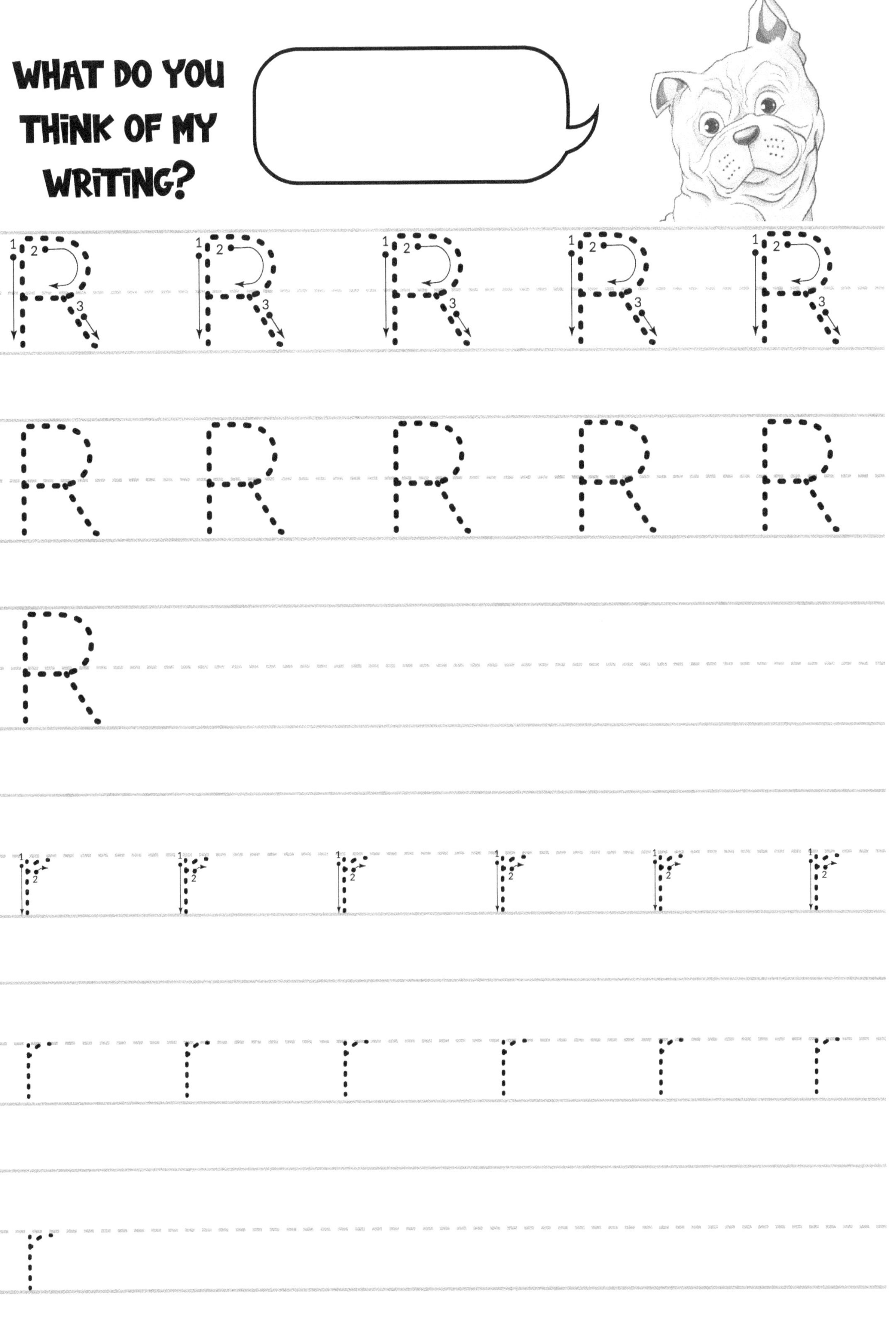

STRAWBERRY

S

Ss

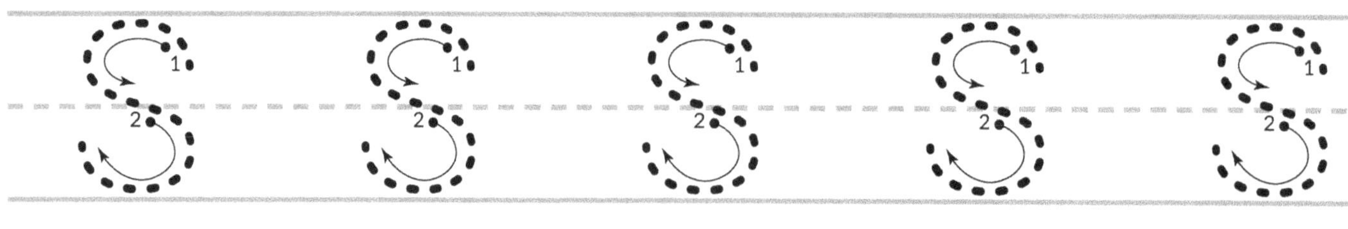

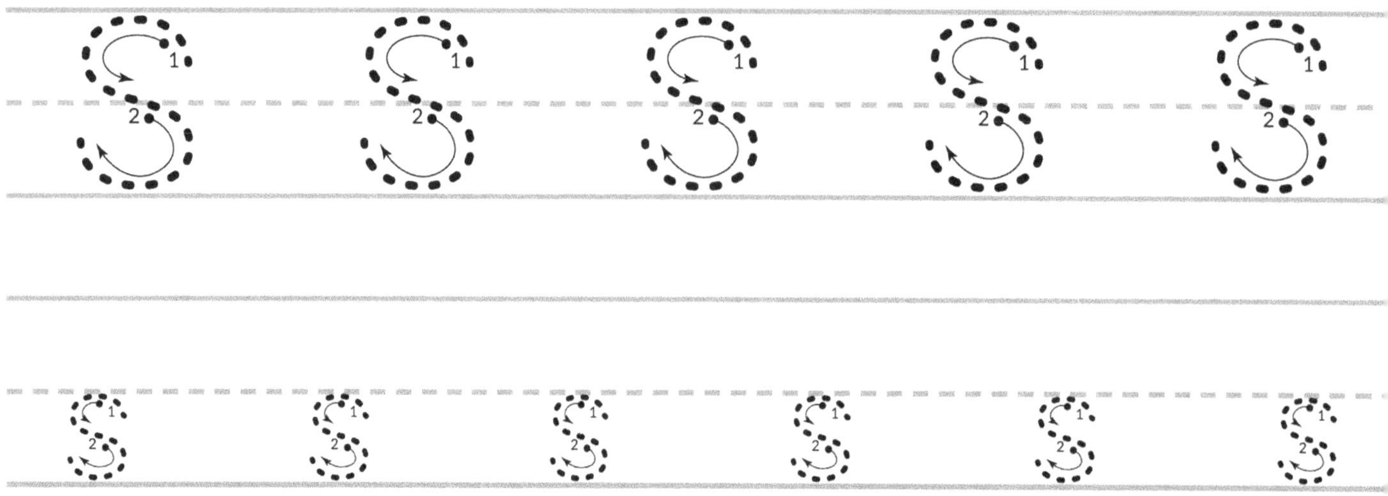

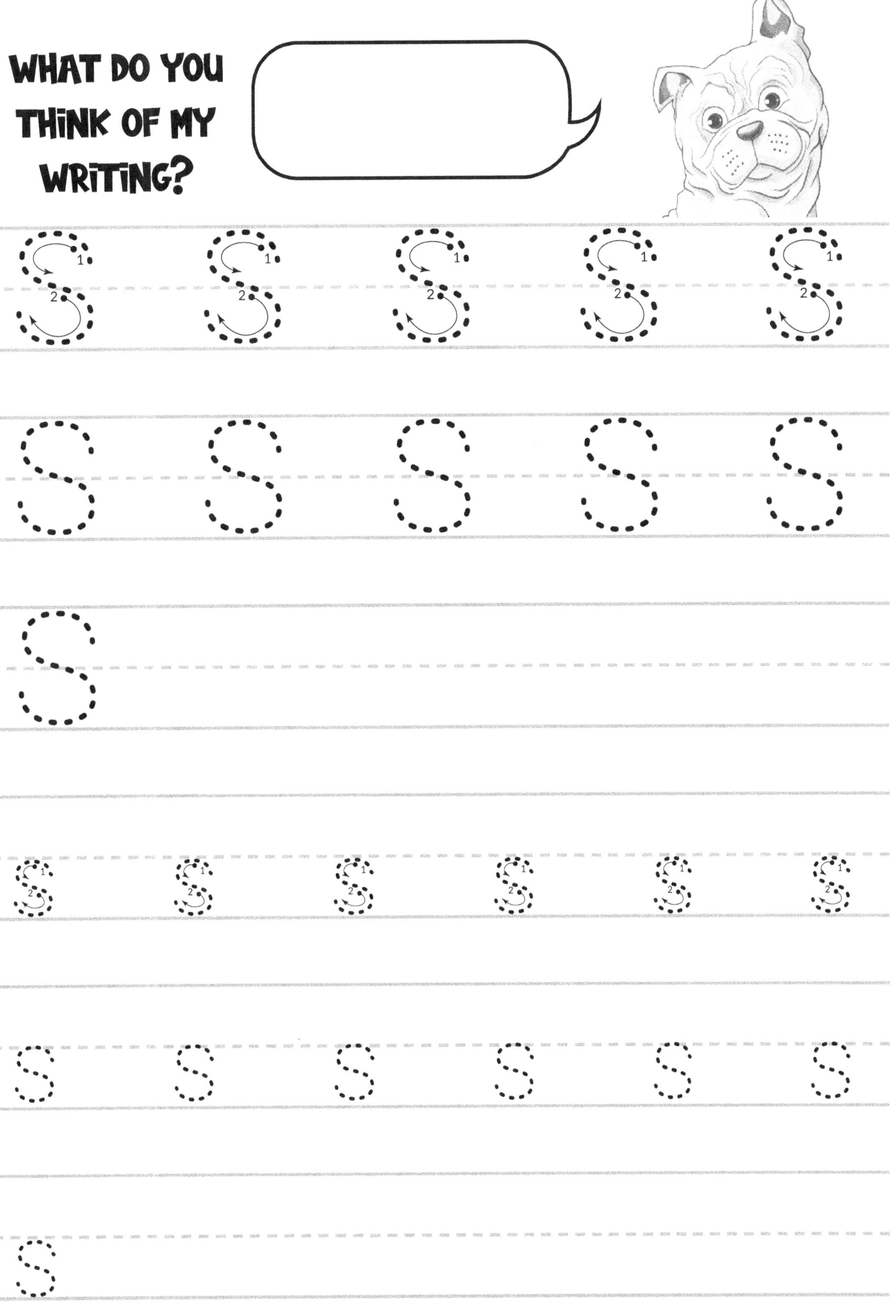

WHAT DO YOU THINK OF MY WRITING?

Tiger
T
Tt

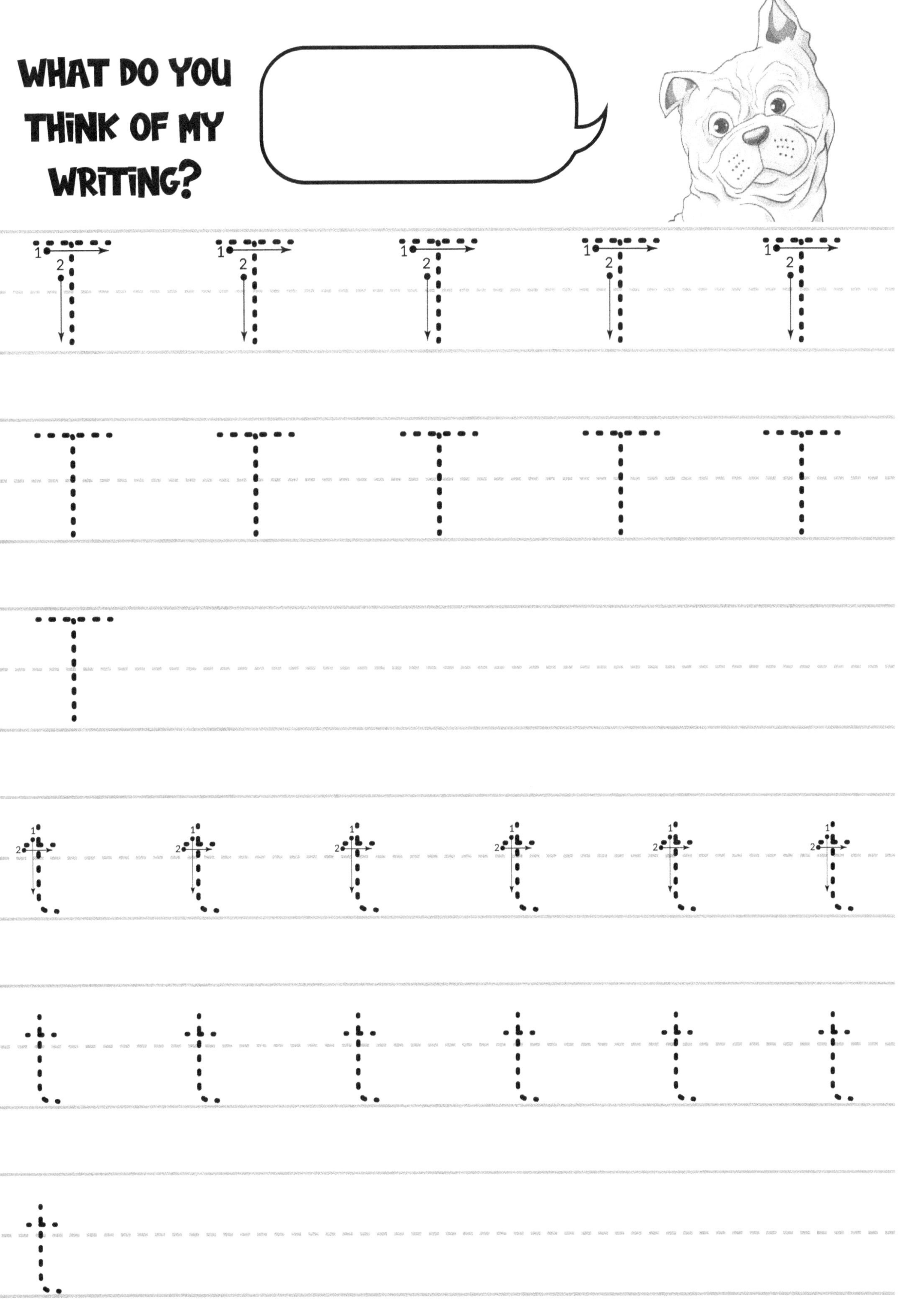

WHAT DO YOU THINK OF MY WRITING?

UMBRELLA

U

Uu

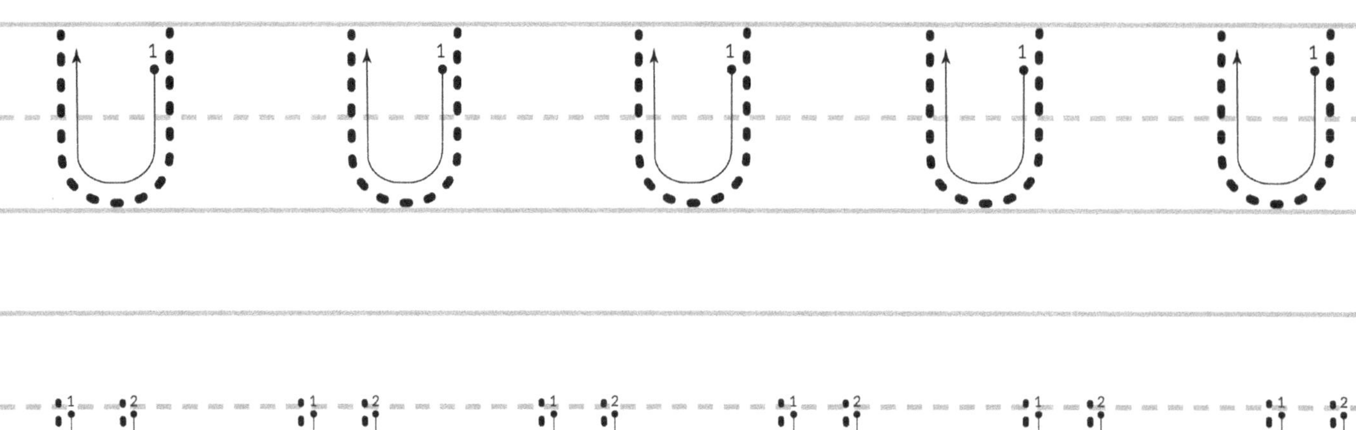

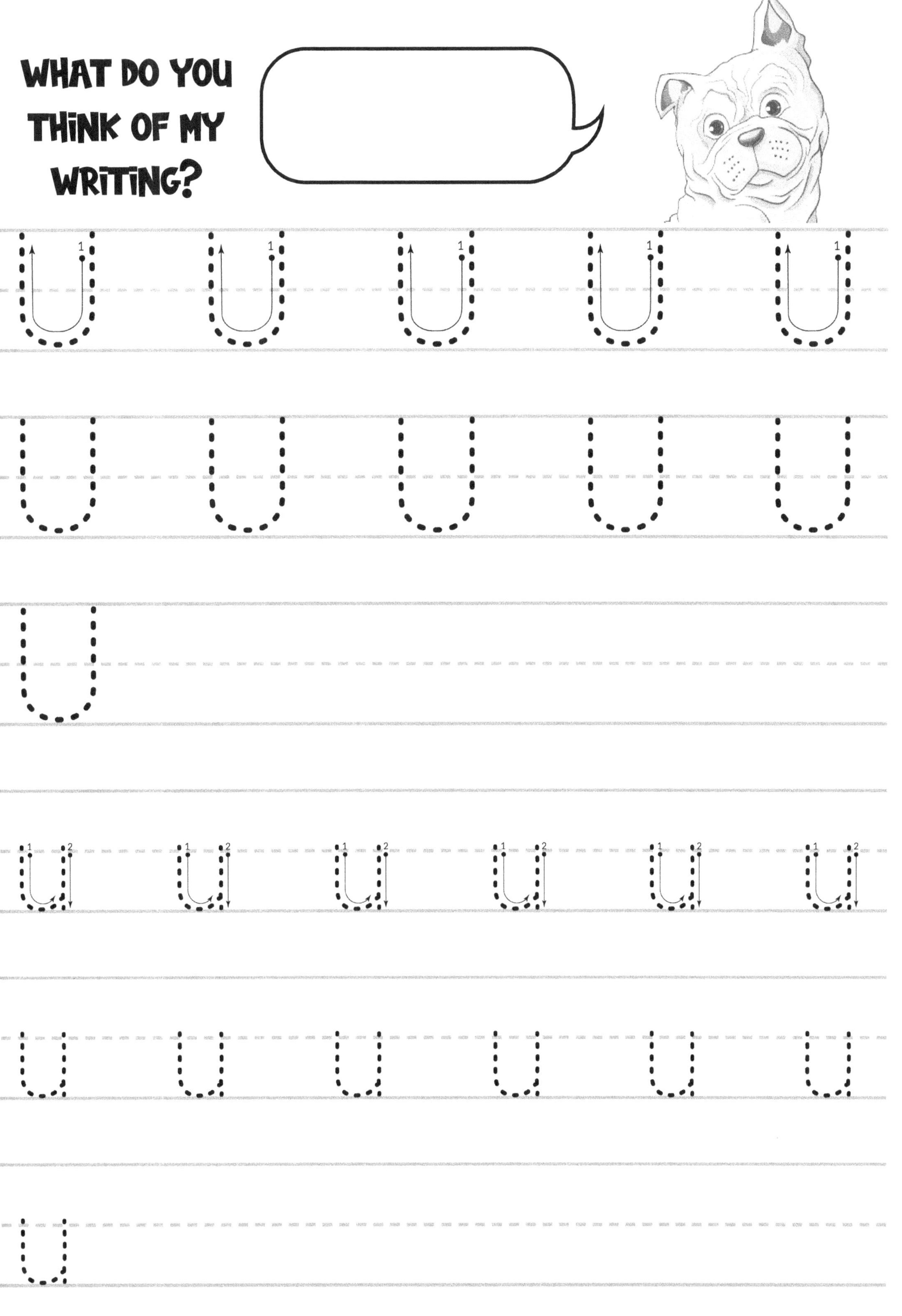

WHAT DO YOU THINK OF MY WRITING?

ViOLiN

V v

Vv

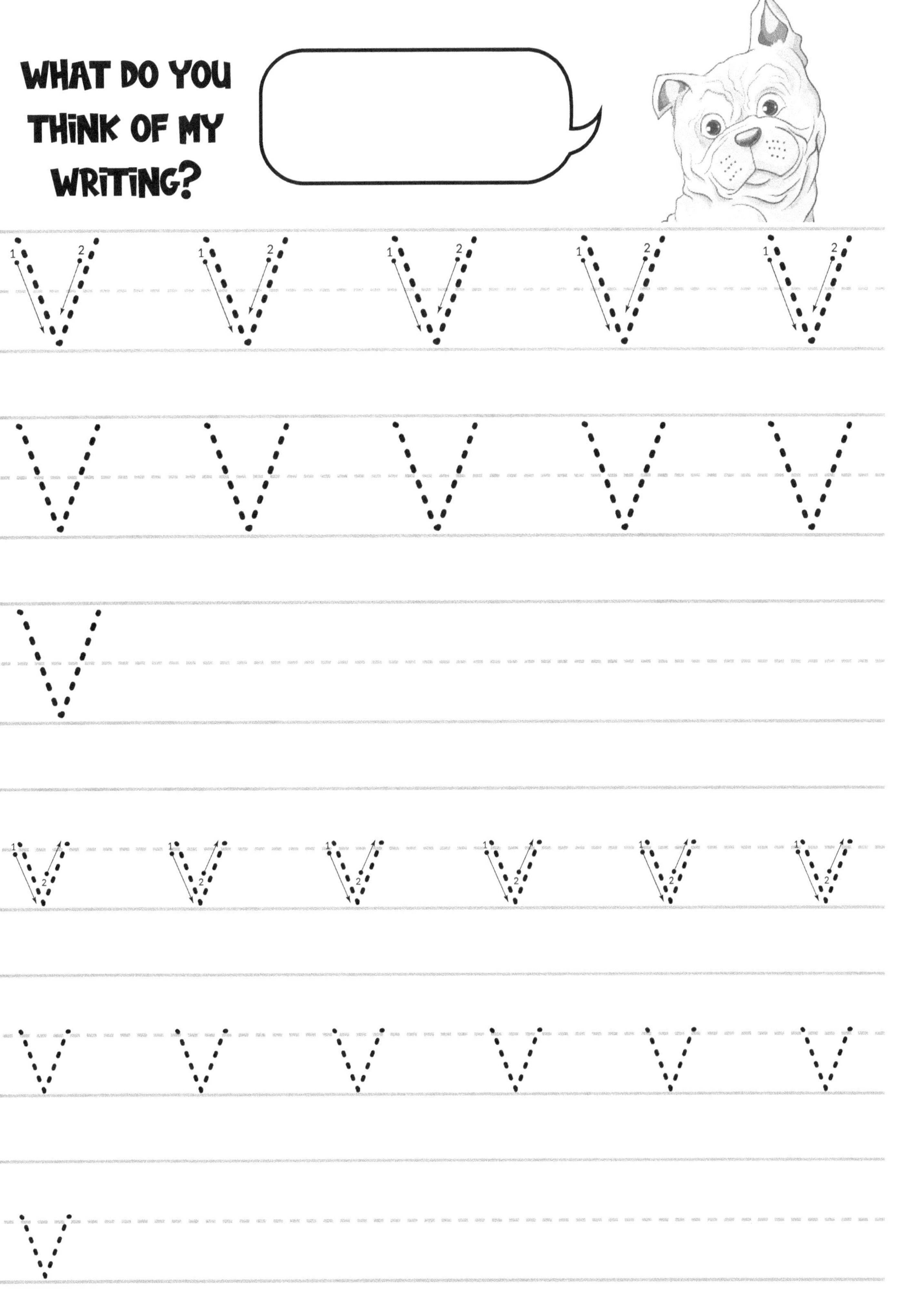

WHAT DO YOU THINK OF MY WRITING?

WATERMELON
W
Ww

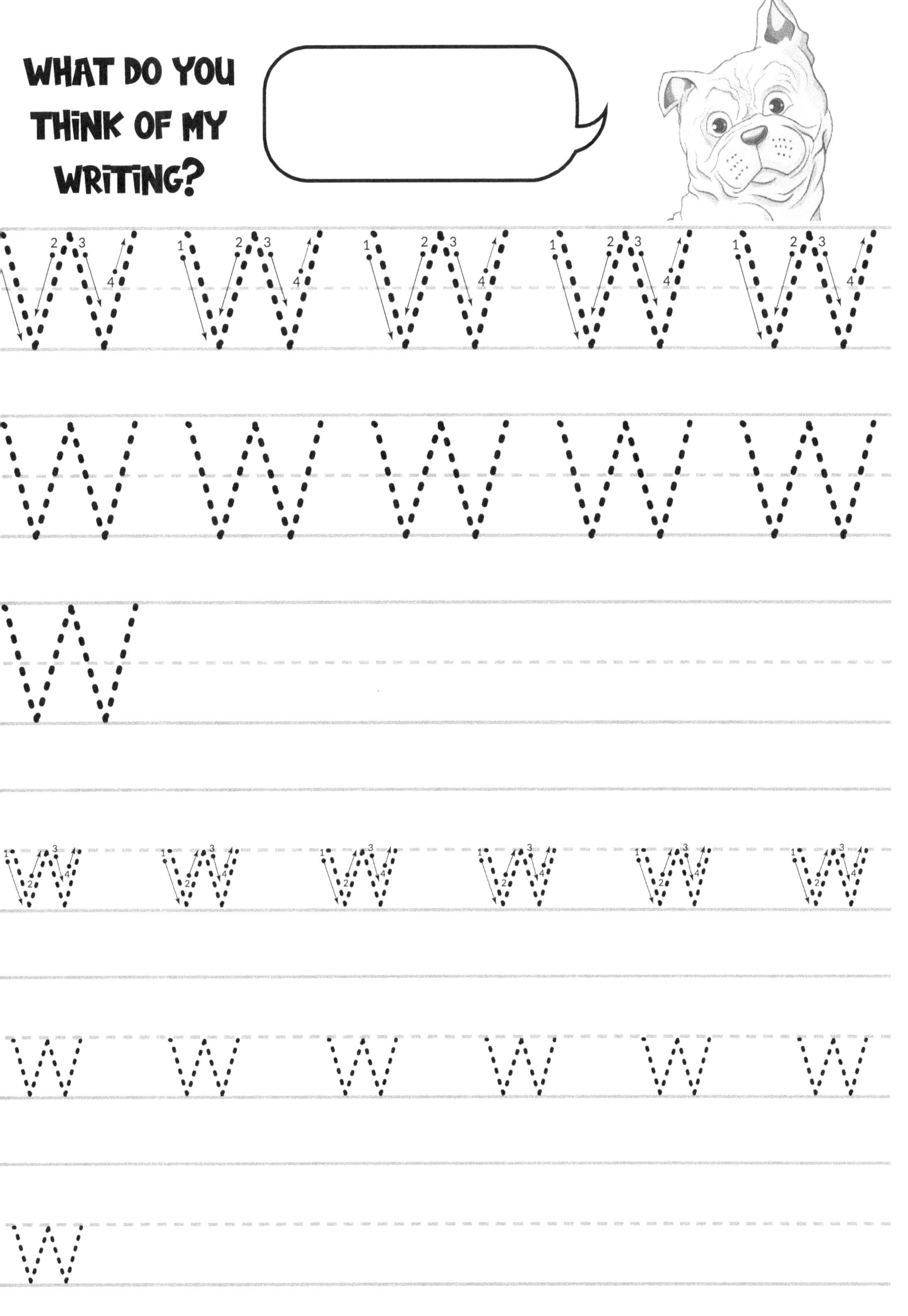

WHAT DO YOU THINK OF MY WRITING?

X-RAY FiSH Xx

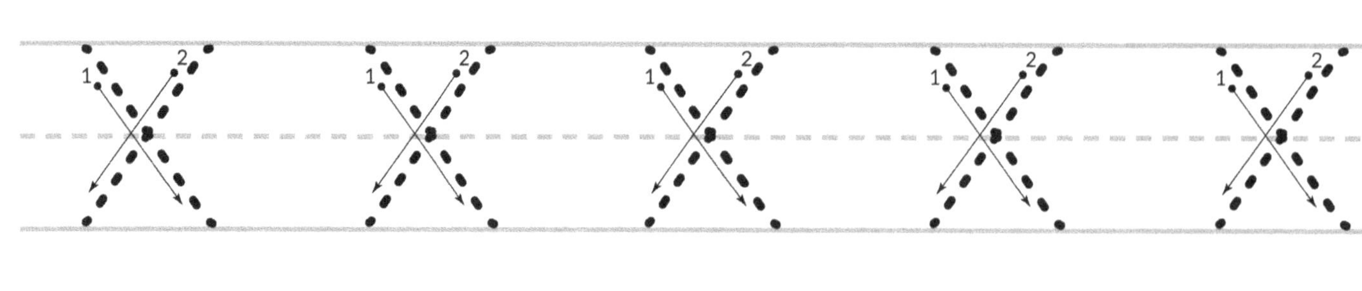

WHAT DO YOU THINK OF MY WRITING?

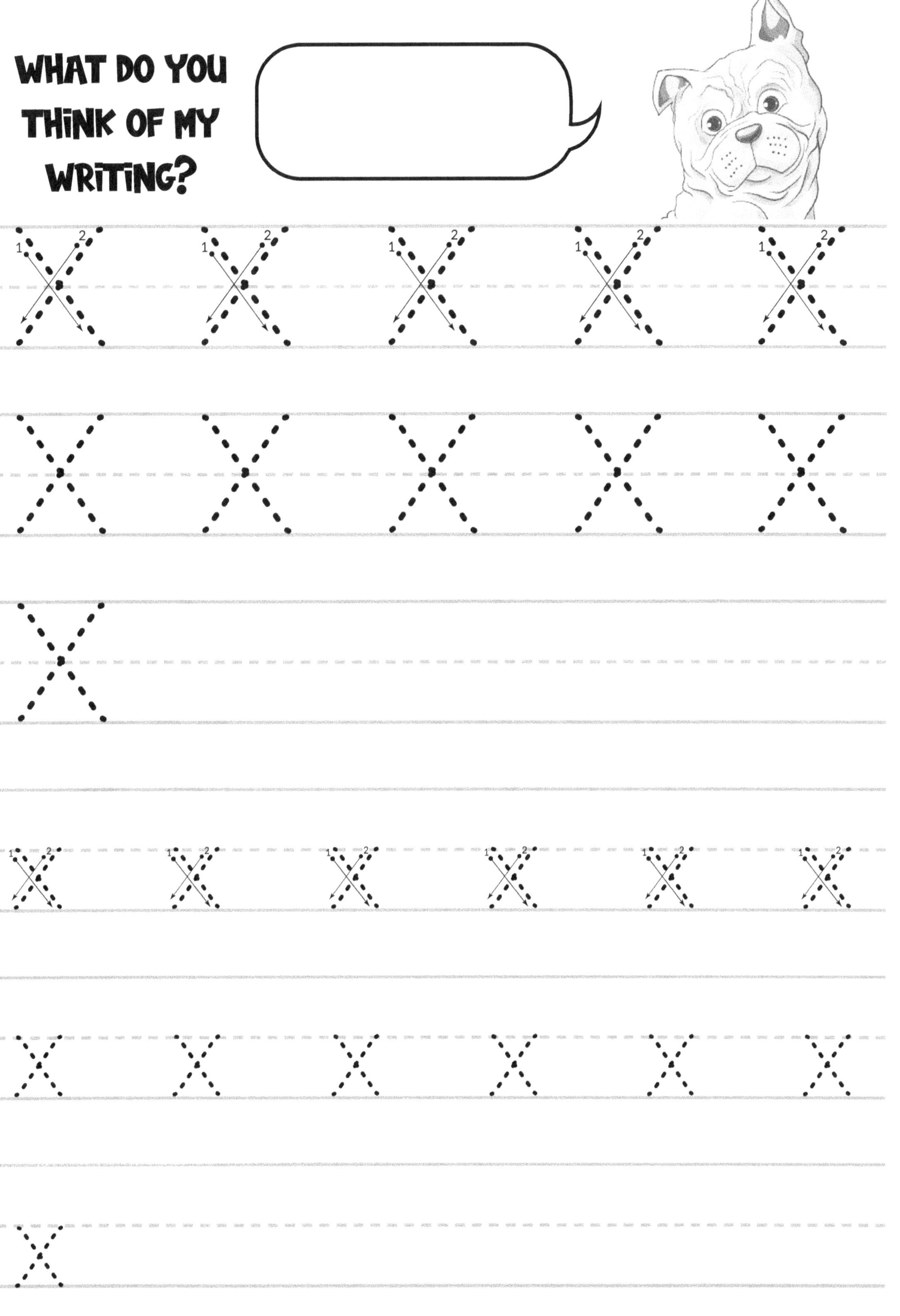

YAK
Y
Yy

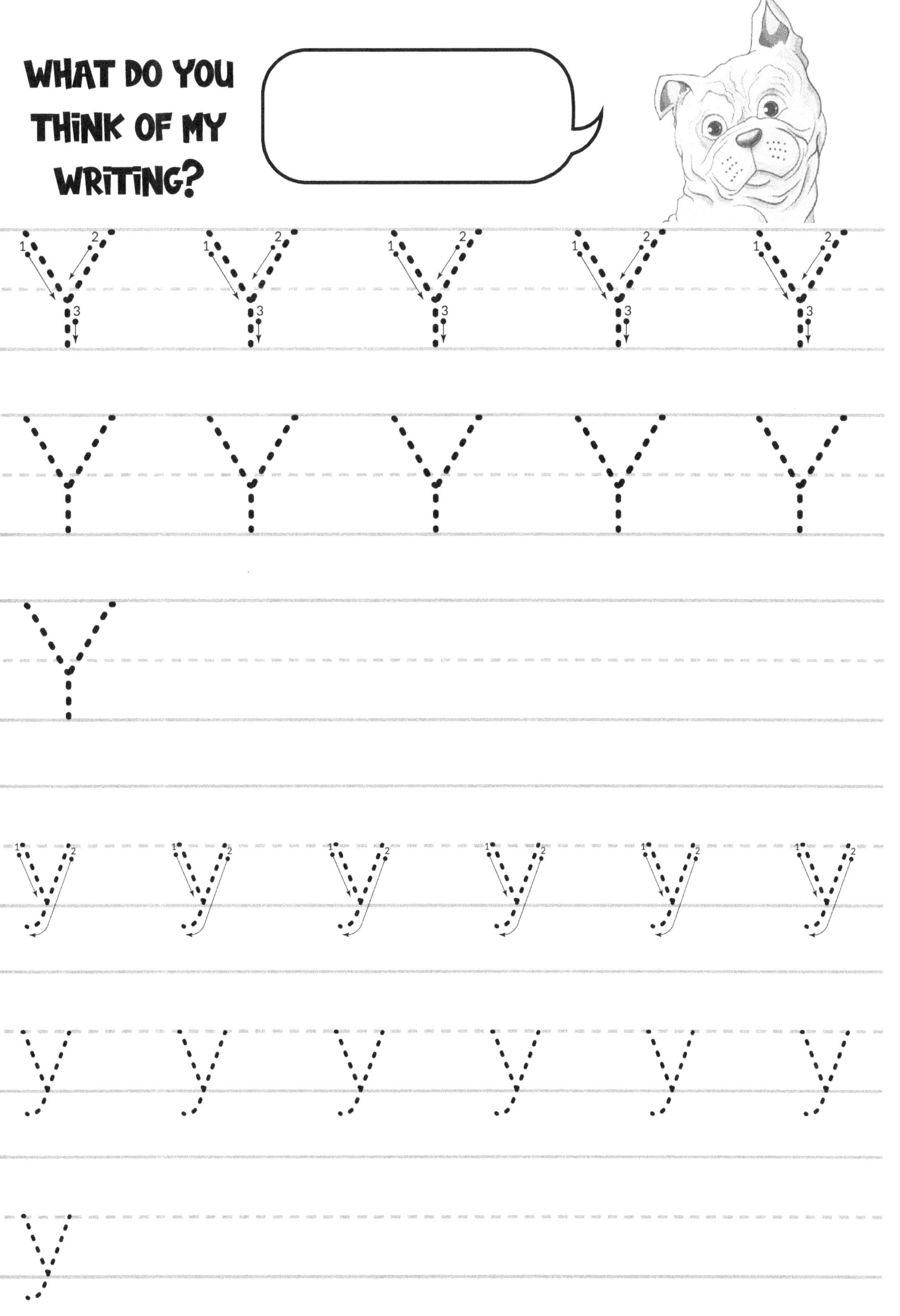

WHAT DO YOU THINK OF MY WRITING?

ZEBRA
Z
Zz

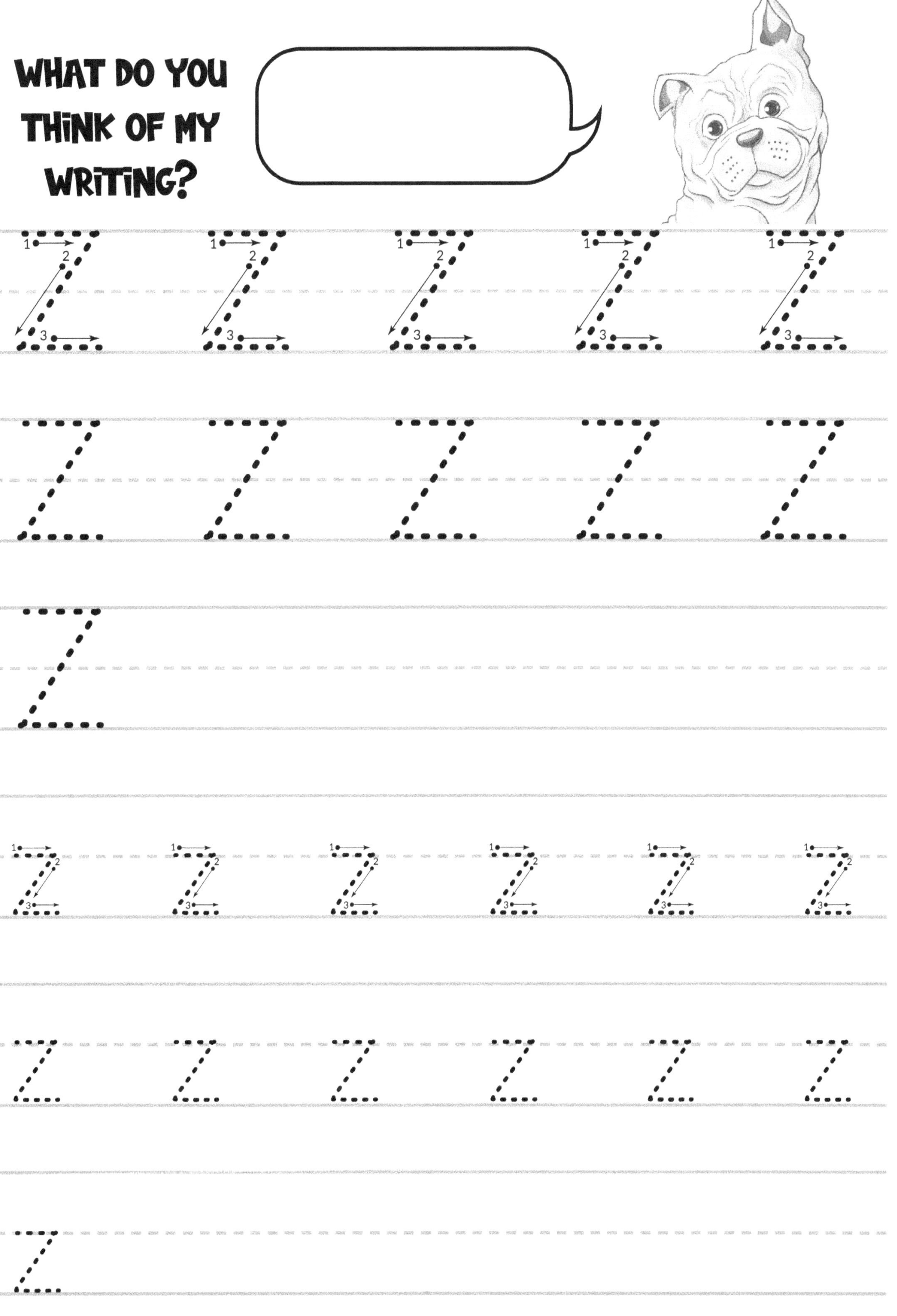

WHAT DO YOU THINK OF MY WRITING?

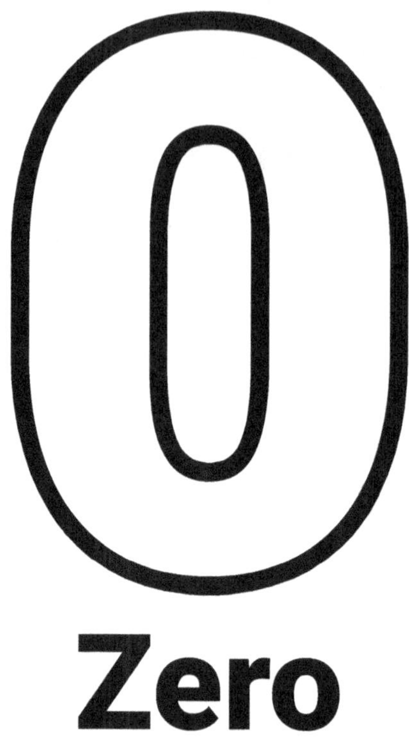

THERE IS _______ ZEBRA.

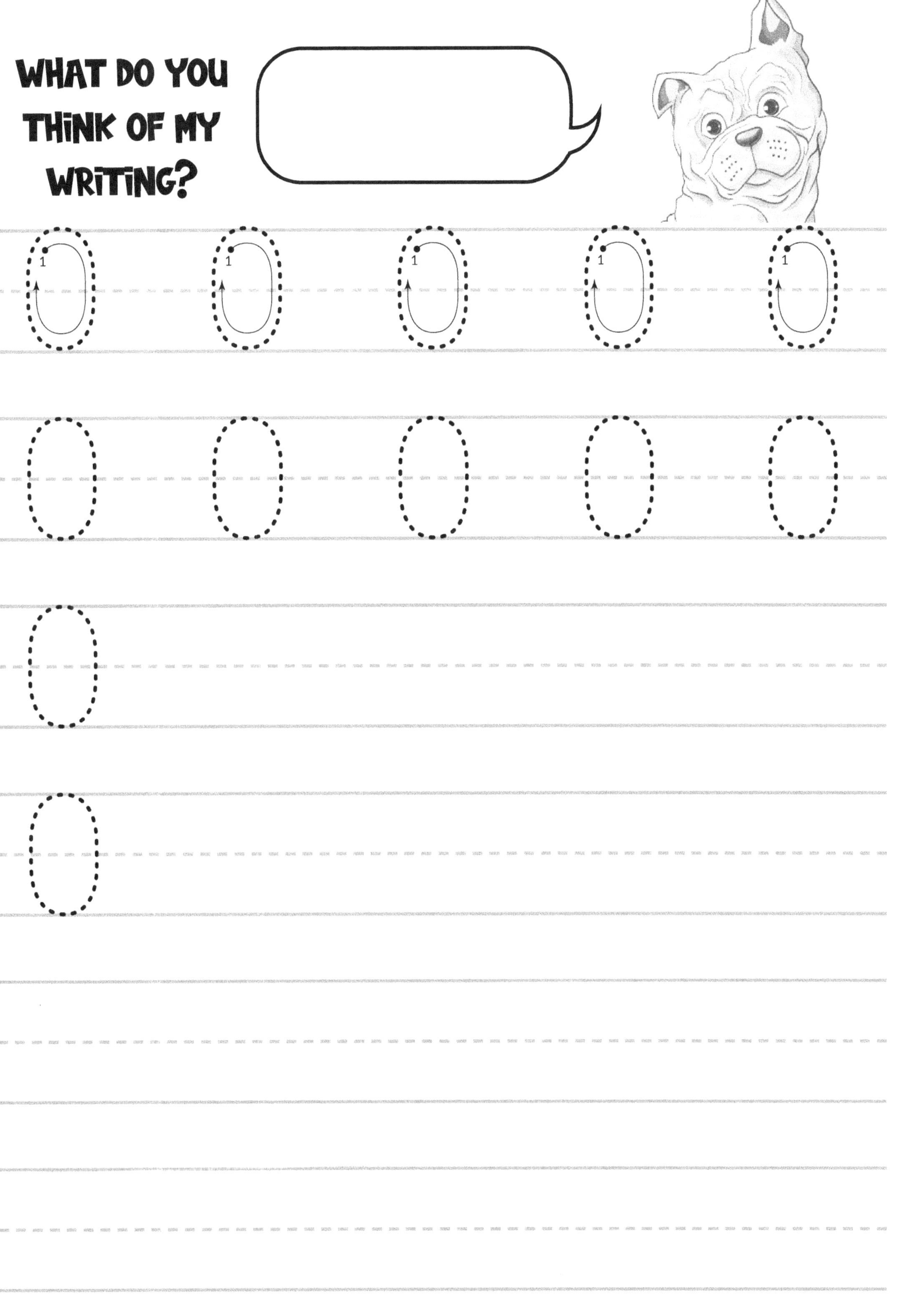

WHAT DO YOU THINK OF MY WRITING?
1
1
1
1
1

One

THERE IS ________ CAT.

WHAT DO YOU THINK OF MY WRITING?

THERE ARE _______ DOGS.

WHAT DO YOU THINK OF MY WRITING?

THERE ARE _______ APPLES.

3 3 3 3 3

3 3 3 3 3

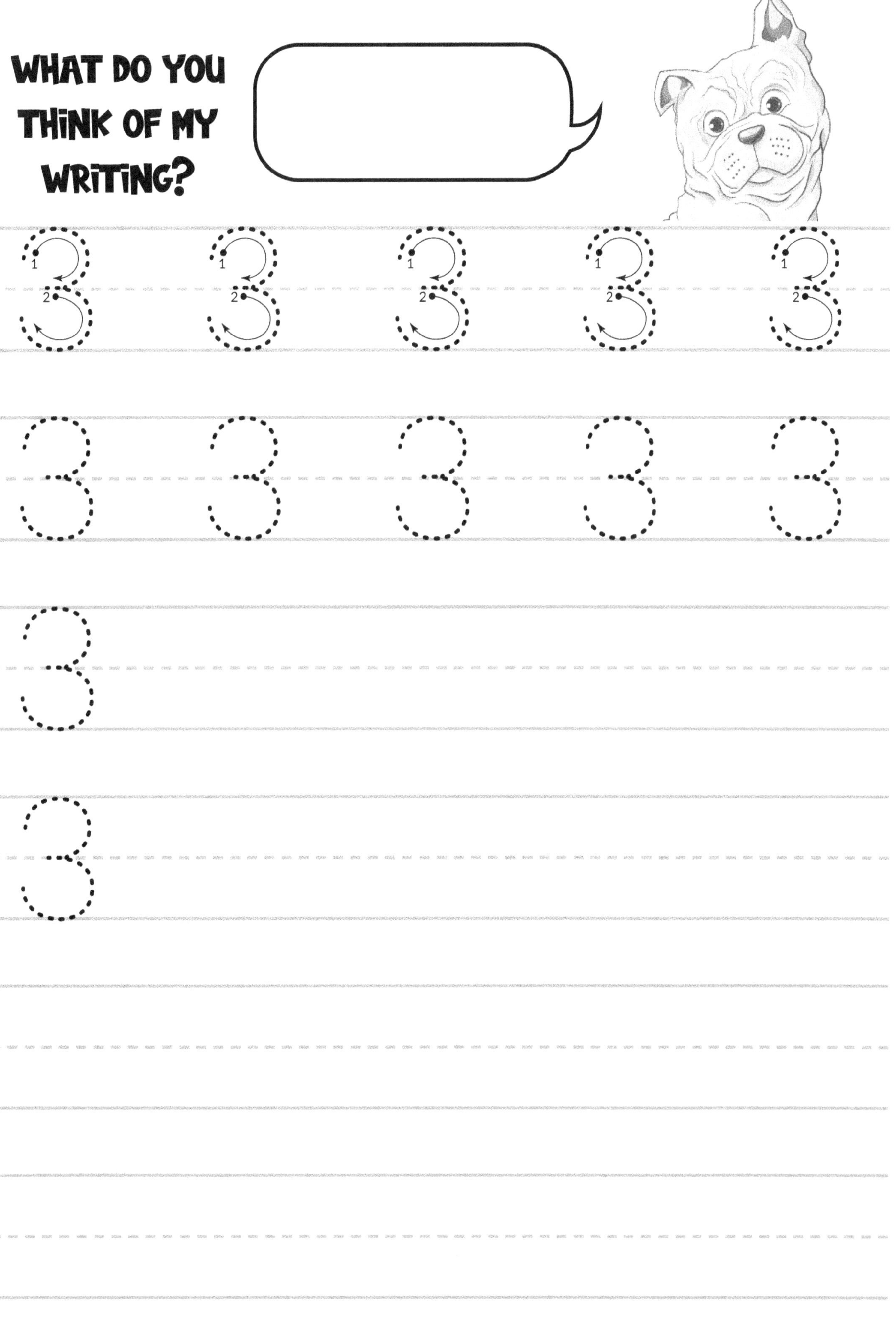

WHAT DO YOU THINK OF MY WRITING?
1
2

4

Four

THERE ARE _______ GOATS.

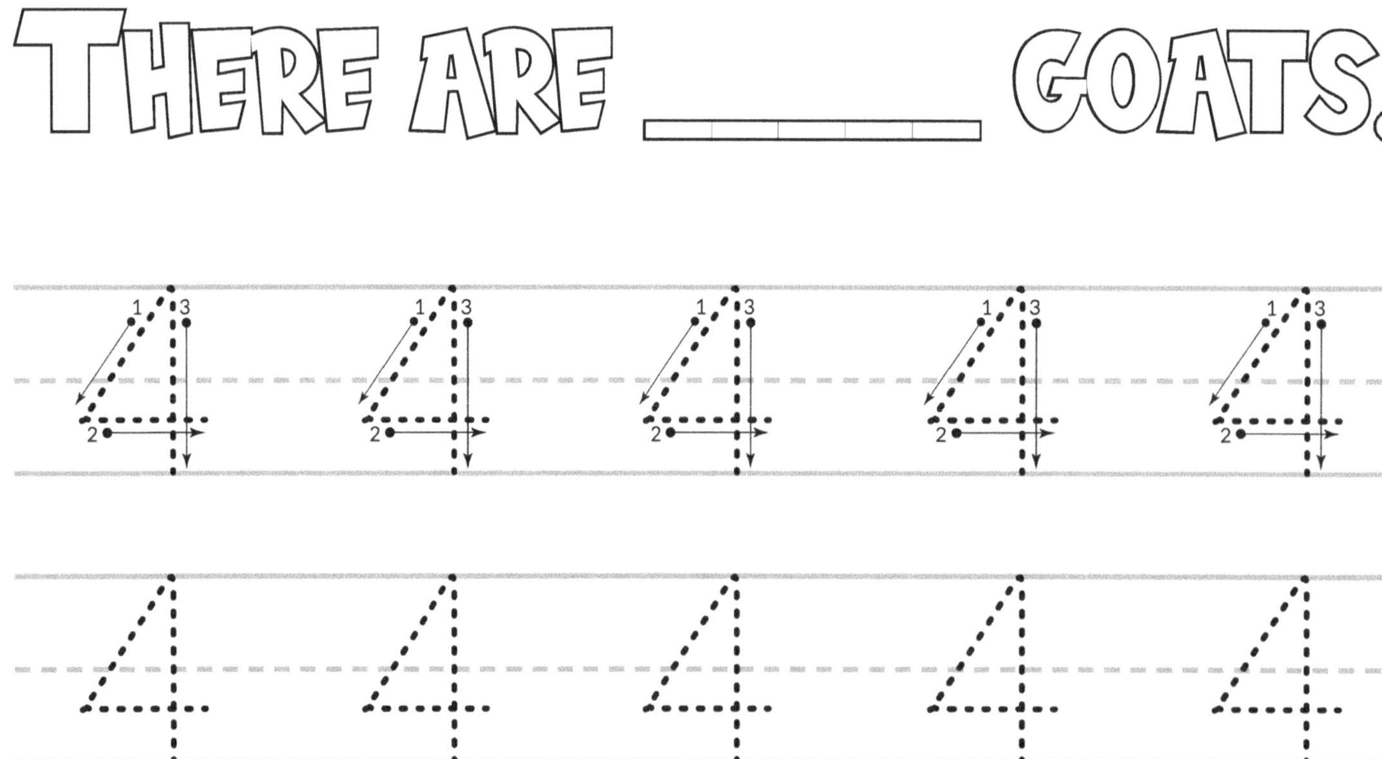

WHAT DO YOU THINK OF MY WRITING?

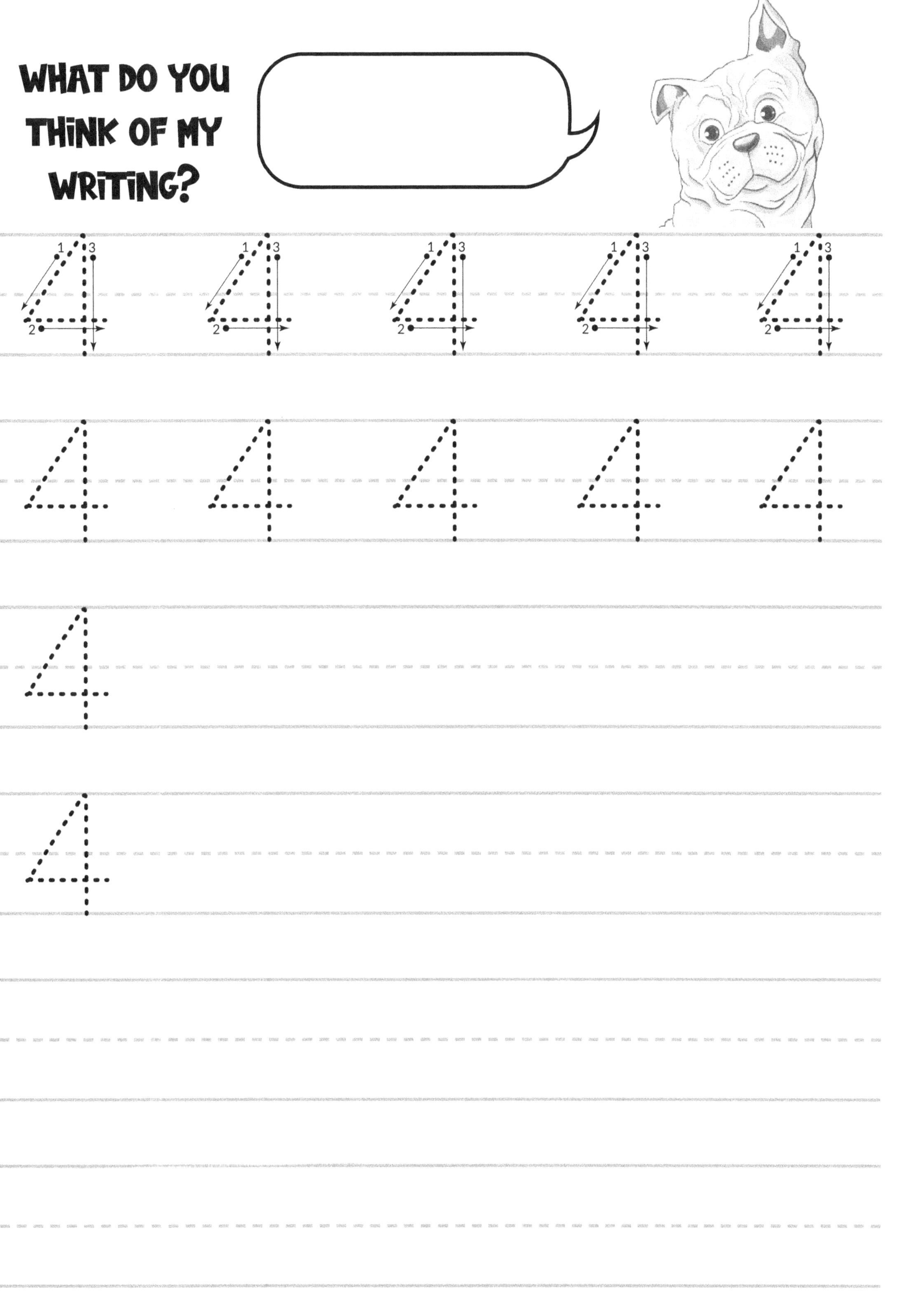

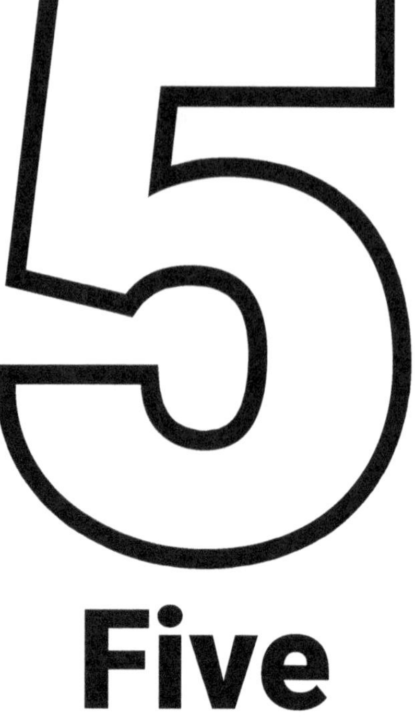

THERE ARE _______ HAMBURGERS.

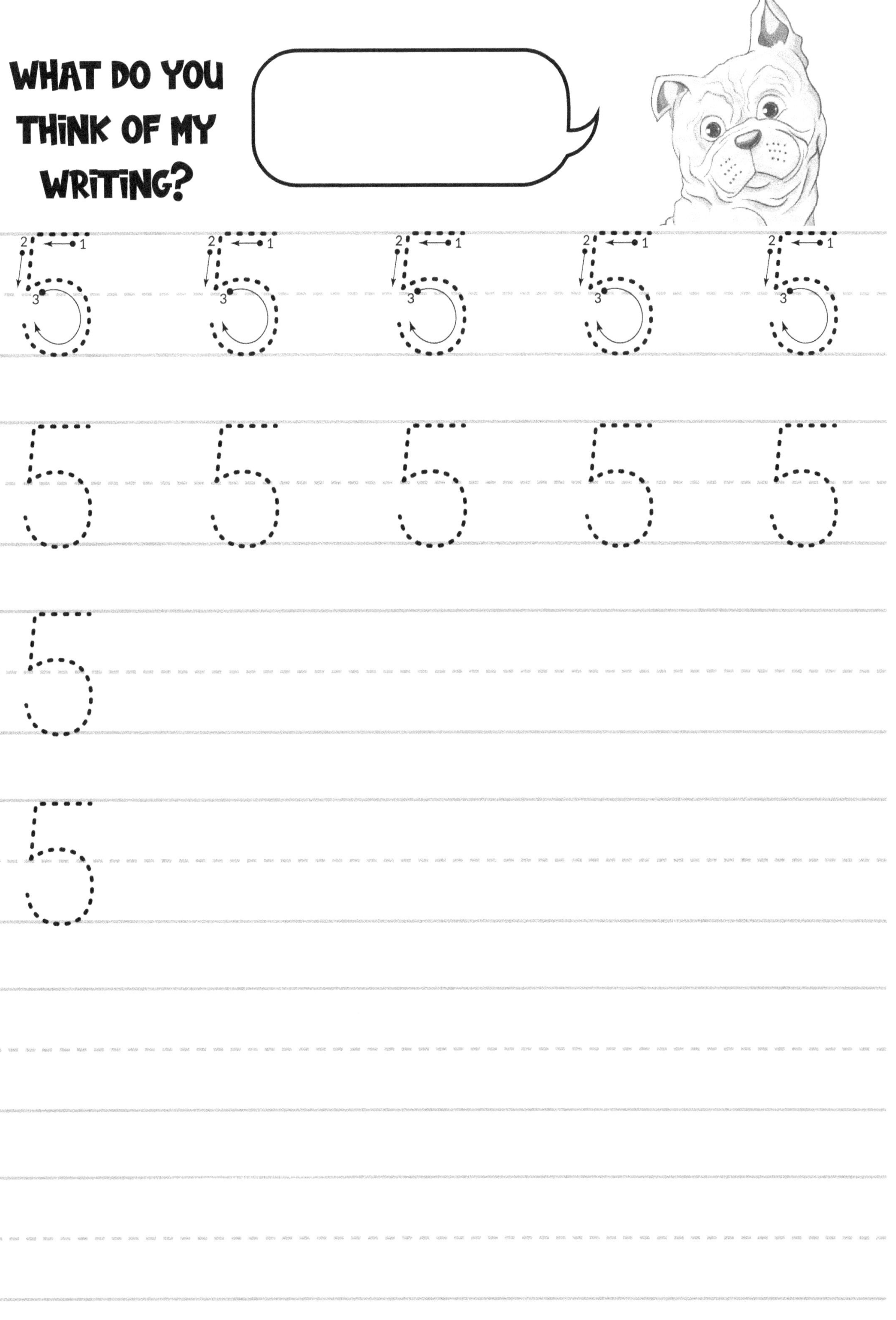

WHAT DO YOU THINK OF MY WRITING?

6

Six

THERE ARE ________ ICE CREAMS.

WHAT DO YOU THINK OF MY WRITING?

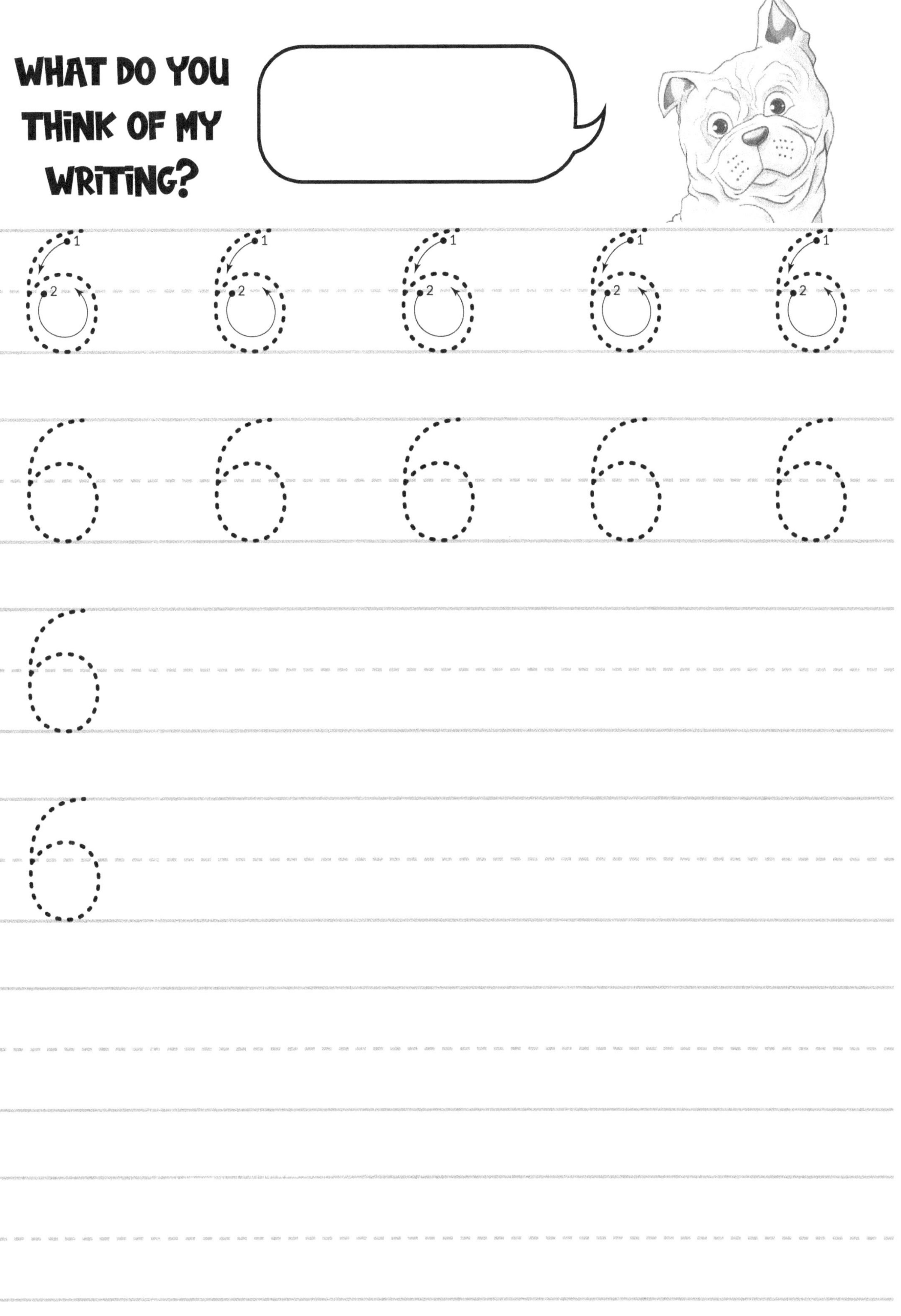

7

SEVEN

THERE ARE _______ MONKEYS.

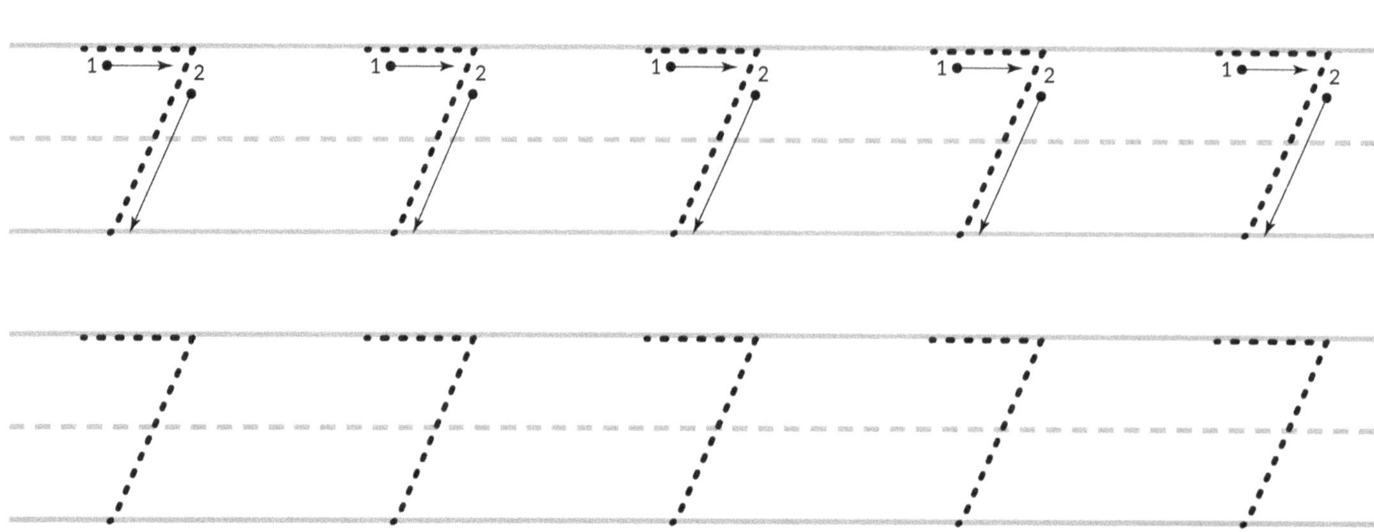

WHAT DO YOU THINK OF MY WRITING?

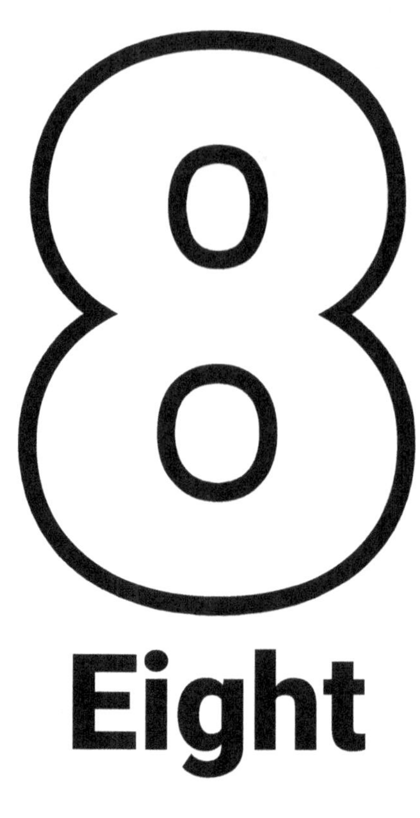

8
Eight

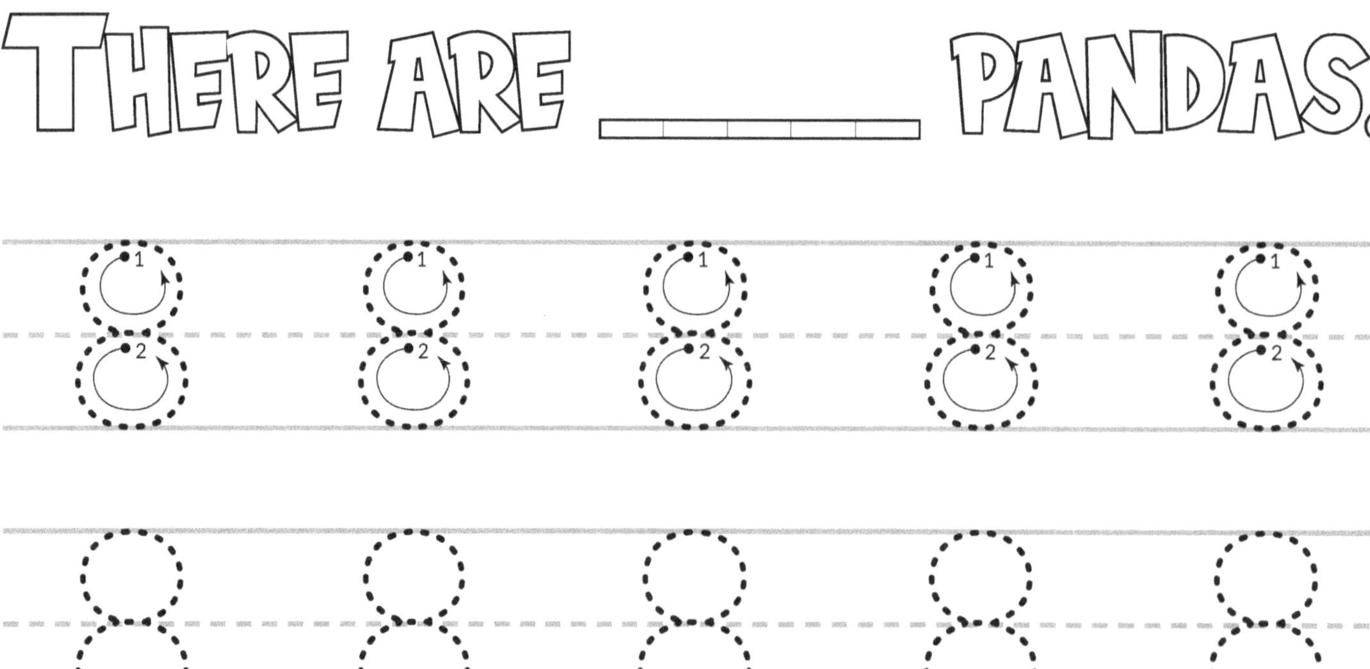

THERE ARE _______ PANDAS.

WHAT DO YOU THINK OF MY WRITING?

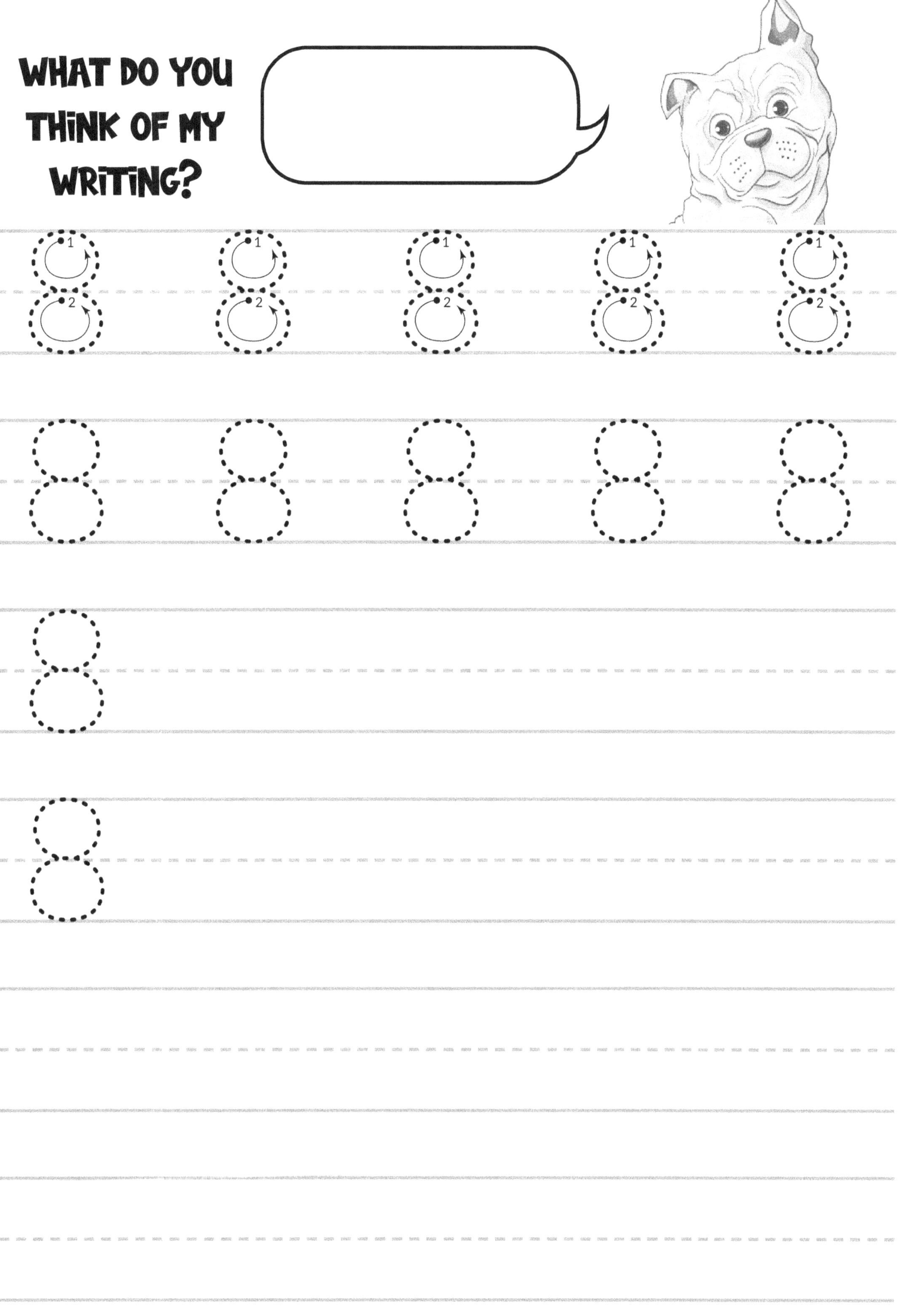

9
Nine

WHAT DO YOU THINK OF MY WRITING?

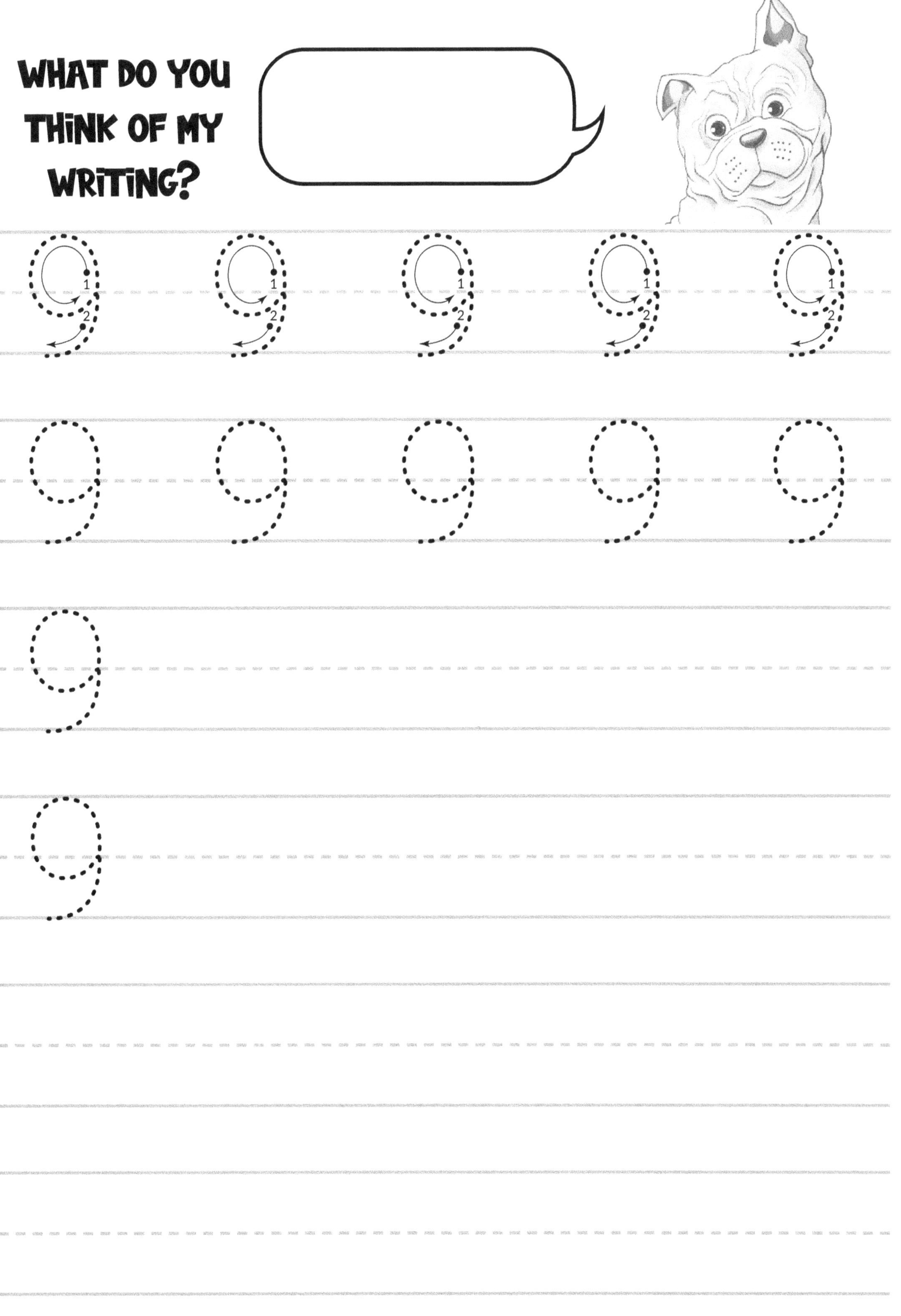

MY NAME IS

(Practice writing your name)

WHAT DO YOU THINK OF MY WRITING?

My Name is

(Practice writing your name)

WHAT DO YOU THINK OF MY WRITING?

MY NAME IS

(Practice writing your name)

WHAT DO YOU THINK OF MY WRITING?

MY NAME iS

(Practice writing your name)

WHAT DO YOU THINK OF MY WRITING?

MY NAME IS

(Practice writing your name)

WHAT DO YOU THINK OF MY WRITING?

MY NAME IS

(Practice writing your name)

WHAT DO YOU THINK OF MY WRITING?

PRACTICE WRITING ANYTHING

WHAT DO YOU THINK OF MY WRITING?

PRACTICE WRITING ANYTHING

WHAT DO YOU THINK OF MY WRITING?

PRACTICE WRITING ANYTHING

WHAT DO YOU THINK OF MY WRITING?

PRACTICE WRITING ANYTHING

WHAT DO YOU THINK OF MY WRITING?

PRACTICE WRITING ANYTHING

WHAT DO YOU THINK OF MY WRITING?

A B C D E F G

H I J K L M N

O P Q R S T U

V W X Y Z

a b c d e f g h i j k l m

n o p q r s t u v w x y z

DIPLOMA

THIS CERTIFICATE IS PRESENTED TO

FOR COMPLETING LEARN TO WRITE ACTIVITY
AND BEING TOTALLY AWESOME

DATE

SIGNATURE